TEACHER'S MANUAL
AND ACHIEVEMENT T...

NORTHSTAR 3
READING AND WRITING
THIRD EDITION

AUTHORS

Laurie Barton

Carolyn Dupaquier Sardinas

SERIES EDITORS

Frances Boyd

Carol Numrich

PEARSON
Longman

**NorthStar: Reading and Writing Level 3, Third Edition
Teacher's Manual and Achievement Tests**

Copyright © 2009, 2004, 1998 by Pearson Education, Inc.
All rights reserved.

Pearson Education, 10 Bank Street, White Plains, NY 10606

Teacher's Manual by Gordon Lewis. Activities for secondary schools by Ann Hilborn.

Achievement Tests developed by Dr. Joan Jamieson and Dr. Carol Chapelle.

Achievement Tests by David Wiese.

Staff credits: The people who made up the *NorthStar: Reading and Writing Level 3, Third Edition Teacher's Manual* team, representing editorial, production, design, and manufacturing, are Dave Dickey, Christine Edmonds, Ann France, Gosia Jaros-White, Dana Klinek, Melissa Leyva, Sherry Preiss, Robert Ruvo, Debbie Sistino, Kathleen Smith, Paula Van Ells, and Adina Zoltan.

Text credits: **Page T-9** From *The Art of the Steal; How to Protect Yourself and Your Business from Fraud—America's #1 Crime* by Frank W. Abagnale, Jr., copyright © 2001 by Frank Abagnale. Used by permission of Broadway Books, a division of Random House, Inc. **Page T-22** Based on information in Deborah Tannen, *You Just Don't Understand: Women and Men in Conversation* (William Morrow and Company, Inc. 1990); **Page T-60 1.** "Facts and Figures on the Death Penalty" (January 1, 2007) as on Amnesty International website. **2-3.** The Gallup Poll, May 2006.

Cover Art: Silvia Rojas/Getty Images
Text composition: ElectraGraphics, Inc.
Text font: 11.5/13 Minion

ISBN-10: 0-13-613369-X
ISBN-13: 978-0-13-613369-8

PEARSON LONGMAN ON THE WEB

Pearsonlongman.com offers online resources for teachers and students. Access our Companion Websites, our online catalog, and our local offices around the world.

Visit us at **www.pearsonlongman.com**.

Printed in the United States of America
4 5 6 7 8 9 10—HAM—13 12 11

CONTENTS

UNIT-BY-UNIT TEACHING SUGGESTIONS

ACHIEVEMENT TESTS

WELCOME TO NORTHSTAR
THIRD EDITION

NorthStar, now in its third edition, motivates students to succeed in their **academic** as well as **personal** language goals.

For each of the five levels, the two strands—*Reading and Writing* and *Listening and Speaking*—provide a fully integrated approach for students and teachers.

WHAT IS SPECIAL ABOUT THE THIRD EDITION?

NEW THEMES

New themes and **updated content**—presented in a **variety of genres**, including literature and lectures, and in **authentic reading and listening selections**—challenge students intellectually.

ACADEMIC SKILLS

More purposeful **integration of critical thinking** and an enhanced focus on **academic skills** such as inferencing, synthesizing, note taking, and test taking help students develop strategies for **success** in the **classroom** and on **standardized tests**. A **culminating productive task** galvanizes content, language, and **critical thinking skills**.

➤ In the *Reading and Writing* strand, a new, **fully integrated writing section** leads students through the **writing process** with engaging writing assignments focusing on various rhetorical modes.

➤ In the *Listening and Speaking* strand, a **structured approach** gives students opportunities for **more extended and creative oral practice**, for example, presentations, simulations, debates, case studies, and public service announcements.

NEW DESIGN

Full **color pages** with more **photos, illustrations, and graphic organizers** foster student engagement and make the content and activities come alive.

MyNorthStarLab

MyNorthStarLab, an easy-to-use **online learning and assessment program**, offers:

➤ Unlimited access to reading and listening selections and DVD segments.

➤ Focused test preparation to help students succeed on international exams such as TOEFL® and IELTS®. Pre- and post-unit assessments improve results by providing individualized instruction, instant feedback, and personalized study plans.

➤ Original activities that support and extend the *NorthStar* program. These include pronunciation practice using voice recording tools, and activities to build note taking skills and academic vocabulary.

➤ Tools that save time. These include a flexible gradebook and authoring features that give teachers control of content and help them track student progress.

THE NORTHSTAR APPROACH

The *NorthStar* series is based on **current research in language acquisition** and on the **experiences of teachers and curriculum designers**. Five principles guide the *NorthStar* approach.

PRINCIPLES

1 The more profoundly students are stimulated intellectually and emotionally, the more language they will use and retain.

The thematic organization of *NorthStar* promotes intellectual and emotional stimulation. The 50 sophisticated themes in *NorthStar* present intriguing topics such as recycled fashion, restorative justice, personal carbon footprints, and microfinance. The authentic content engages students, links them to language use outside of the classroom, and encourages personal expression and critical thinking.

2 Students can learn both the form and content of the language.

Grammar, vocabulary, and culture are inextricably woven into the units, providing students with systematic and multiple exposures to language forms in a variety of contexts. As the theme is developed, students can express complex thoughts using a higher level of language.

3 Successful students are active learners.

Tasks are designed to be creative, active, and varied. Topics are interesting and up-to-date. Together these tasks and topics (1) allow teachers to bring the outside world into the classroom and (2) motivate students to apply their classroom learning in the outside world.

4 Students need feedback.

This feedback comes naturally when students work together practicing language and participating in open-ended opinion and inference tasks. Whole class activities invite teachers' feedback on the spot or via audio/video recordings or notes. The innovative new MyNorthStarLab gives students immediate feedback as they complete computer-graded language activities online; it also gives students the opportunity to submit writing or speaking assignments electronically to their instructor for feedback later.

5 The quality of relationships in the language classroom is important because students are asked to express themselves on issues and ideas.

The information and activities in *NorthStar* promote genuine interaction, acceptance of differences, and authentic communication. By building skills and exploring ideas, the exercises help students participate in discussions and write essays of an increasingly complex and sophisticated nature.

THE NORTHSTAR UNIT

1 FOCUS ON THE TOPIC

This section introduces students to the unifying theme of the reading selections.

> **PREDICT** and **SHARE INFORMATION** foster interest in the unit topic and help students develop a personal connection to it.
>
> **BACKGROUND** AND **VOCABULARY** activities provide students with tools for understanding the first reading selection. Later in the unit, students review this vocabulary and learn related idioms, collocations, and word forms. This helps them explore content and expand their written and spoken language.

UNIT 9

Is Our Climate Changing?

1 FOCUS ON THE TOPIC

A PREDICT

Look at the photograph of the Earth. Discuss the questions in a small group.

1. What are some ways in which the Earth is changing?
2. How responsible are humans for changes on the planet?
3. Are these changes making the world better or worse?

163

B SHARE INFORMATION

*Write **A** (agree) or **D** (disagree) next to each statement. Discuss your answers with a classmate.*

_____ 1. The Earth goes through warming and cooling periods, and the warming period happening now is just part of those natural changes.

_____ 2. The weather has become more dangerous in recent years.

_____ 3. The hole in the ozone layer[1] is causing climate change.

_____ 4. New fuels will solve the problem of pollution.

_____ 5. Some people are frightening us with "global warming" so they can make money from it.

[1] **ozone layer:** a layer of ozone above the Earth that prevents harmful radiation from the sun reaching the Earth's surface

C BACKGROUND AND VOCABULARY

1 *Look at the pictures and read the texts. Pay special attention to the boldfaced words.*

How Greenhouse Gases Cause Climate Change

Most of the sun's heat hits the Earth and **escapes** back into space. Some is trapped by the **atmosphere** and warms the Earth.

Fossil fuels (coal, gasoline) are burned and **carbon dioxide** (CO_2) is released. Released CO_2 and other **gases** are called greenhouse gas **emissions**.

Greenhouse gases make the atmosphere thicker. As the sun's heat hits the Earth, more and more of the heat is trapped and warms the Earth. As CO_2 increases, so does the temperature. This shows that there is a **link** between CO_2 and temperature. This connection is **evidence** that climate change is caused by humans.

164   UNIT 9

2 FOCUS ON READING

This section focuses on understanding two contrasting reading selections.

> **READING ONE** is a literary selection, academic article, news piece, blog, or other genre that addresses the unit topic. In levels 1 to 3, readings are based on authentic materials. In levels 4 and 5, all the readings are authentic.
>
> **READ FOR MAIN IDEAS** and **READ FOR DETAILS** are comprehension activities that lead students to an understanding and appreciation of the first selection.

2 FOCUS ON READING

A READING ONE: Our Climate Is Changing ...

Read the article adapted from a New Zealand government brochure.

Our Climate is Changing and It is Going to Keep Changing

Climate Change

1   It's getting hotter. Our climate is changing, so you'd better get used to it. It's changing because of what we humans do and the **gases** we have put into the atmosphere. We have already put so much gas into the atmosphere, the climate will keep changing for a long, long time. Some of the changes may be good (at least in the short term) and some may be bad. But change is a near certainty.

2   We have known for 25 years that the atmosphere was changing. The most obvious **sign** was an increase in **carbon dioxide** (CO_2), the gas we breathe out and the gas produced when we burn **fossil fuels** such as coal and gasoline. This is the same gas that is absorbed by plants to make food. Before 1900 the amount of carbon dioxide in the atmosphere was 270 to 280 parts per million (ppm). Now it has grown to 380 parts per million. In the same time, the world has become steadily hotter. It is this **link**, this connection, that tells us that carbon dioxide is causing the warming. This **evidence** is powerful proof that humans, not nature, are causing climate change.

Not Just Hotter

3   Since the atmosphere is getting hotter, it is also getting more **energetic**. This means that in some places it will be windier, in some places wetter, in some places drier. In some places it may even be cooler. That's why we talk about "climate change" rather than "global warming." Although on average it will be warmer, it won't necessarily be warmer everywhere.

Can We Stop It?

4   No. We can slow it, but we can't stop it for a long, long time. We have already made the greenhouse gas **emissions** that will keep the atmosphere changing for decades to come. If we could keep the world's greenhouse gas emissions from growing, the temperature would continue to grow as fast as it is growing now. If we could cut emissions by half, the world would still keep getting hotter for a hundred years or more. But if we act soon, we can make sure the changes can be managed and kept to a minimum, and we can **adapt** to them.

(continued on next page)

READ FOR MAIN IDEAS

*Write **T** (true) or **F** (false) for each statement.*

_____ 1. Tony Hawk is ashamed of his occupation.

_____ 2. He wants all his skateboard tricks to be perfect.

_____ 3. His classmates liked him because of his skateboarding ability.

_____ 4. His parents thought that skateboarding was a waste of time.

_____ 5. He had a smooth and flowing style.

_____ 6. He earned a lot of money before the age of 25.

READ FOR DETAILS

Write one-sentence answers to the questions. Then compare answers with a partner.

1. What did Tony Hawk achieve at the 1999 Summer X Games?
   _____

2. How much time did he spend practicing his most famous trick?
   _____

3. When did he begin skateboarding?
   _____

4. Where did he learn to ride a skateboard?
   _____

5. What kind of problems did he have in school?
   _____

6. Who saw Tony's tricks in a Tarzan movie?
   _____

MAKE INFERENCES

Decide which of the statements can be inferred from Reading One. Check (✓) the correct answers. Refer to the reading to find support for your answers. Compare your answers with a partner.

_____ 1. Baggy skater clothes weren't popular at Tony's first school.

_____ 2. Tony didn't try difficult tricks at first.

_____ 3. Tony's parents married late in life.

_____ 4. The principal at Tony's first school didn't support his skateboarding.

_____ 5. Tony got excellent grades at his second school.

_____ 6. At Tony's second school, he was popular with the other students.

> Following this comprehension section, the **MAKE INFERENCES** activity prompts students to "read between the lines," move beyond the literal meaning, exercise critical thinking skills, and understand the text on a more academic level. Students follow up with pair or group work to discuss topics in the **EXPRESS OPINIONS** section.

READING TWO offers another perspective on the topic and usually belongs to another genre. Again, in levels 1 to 3, the readings are based on authentic materials, and in levels 4 and 5, they are authentic. This second reading is followed by an activity that challenges students to question ideas they formed about the first reading, and to use appropriate language skills to analyze and explain their ideas.

INTEGRATE READINGS ONE AND TWO presents culminating activities. Students are challenged to take what they have learned, organize the information, and synthesize it in a meaningful way. Students practice skills that are essential for success in authentic academic settings and on standardized tests.

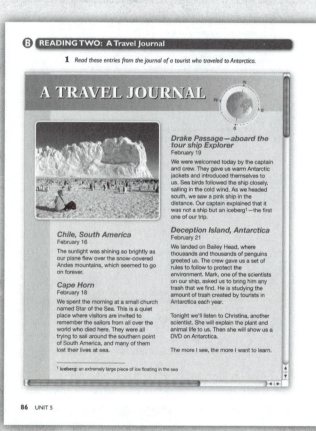

B **READING TWO: A Travel Journal**

1 *Read these entries from the journal of a tourist who traveled to Antarctica.*

A TRAVEL JOURNAL

Drake Passage—aboard the tour ship Explorer
February 19

We were welcomed today by the captain and crew. They gave us warm Antarctic jackets and introduced themselves to us. Sea birds followed the ship closely, sailing in the cold wind. As we headed south, we saw a pink ship in the distance. Our captain explained that it was not a ship but an iceberg[1]—the first one of our trip.

Chile, South America
February 16

The sunlight was shining so brightly as our plane flew over the snow-covered Andes mountains, which seemed to go on forever.

Cape Horn
February 18

We spent the morning at a small church named Star of the Sea. This is a quiet place where visitors are invited to remember the sailors from all over the world who died here. They were all trying to sail around the southern point of South America, and many of them lost their lives at sea.

Deception Island, Antarctica
February 21

We landed on Bailey Head, where thousands and thousands of penguins greeted us. The crew gave us a set of rules to follow to protect the environment. Mark, one of the scientists on our ship, asked us to bring him any trash that we find. He is studying the amount of trash created by tourists in Antarctica each year.

Tonight we'll listen to Christina, another scientist. She will explain the plant and animal life to us. Then she will show us a DVD on Antarctica.

The more I see, the more I want to learn.

[1] **iceberg:** an extremely large piece of ice floating in the sea

C **INTEGRATE READINGS ONE AND TWO**

STEP 1: Organize

Below is a list of characteristics and a Venn Diagram. Put characteristics that describe Tony Hawk in the left circle, characteristics that describe Ashley Lindermann in the right circle, and those that describe both athletes in the middle part where the two circles overlap.

Characteristics

Competitive
Dedicated
Desire to be the best
Need to feel in control
Life of pressure
World seems scary
Family is supportive
Family adds pressure
Obsession leads to success
Obsession leads to anorexia
Obsession helps to escape pain

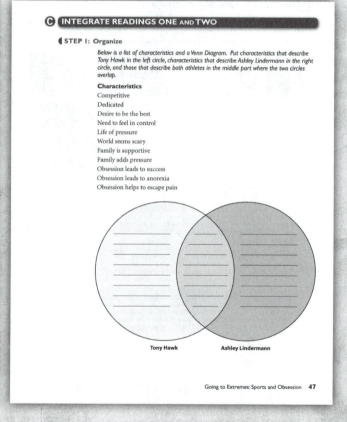

Tony Hawk   Ashley Lindermann

③ FOCUS ON WRITING

This section emphasizes development of productive skills for writing. It includes sections on vocabulary, grammar, and the writing process.

The **VOCABULARY** section leads students from reviewing the unit vocabulary, to practicing and expanding their use of it, and then working with it—using it creatively in both this section and in the final writing task.

Students learn useful structures for writing in the **GRAMMAR** section, which offers a concise presentation and targeted practice. Vocabulary items are recycled here, providing multiple exposures leading to mastery. For additional practice with the grammar presented, students and teachers can consult the GRAMMAR BOOK REFERENCES at the end of the book for corresponding material in the *Focus on Grammar* and Azar series.

---

③ FOCUS ON WRITING

Ⓐ VOCABULARY

◀ REVIEW

Read the paragraph about traditional courtship. Then, decide if the sentences below are related to courtship (C), the wedding ceremony (W), or married life (M), and mark them appropriately. Share your choices with the class.

> **Courtship** refers to the period of time when a man and a woman get to know each other before marriage. In some cultures, they spend time together alone. In other cultures, they spend time together with friends and relatives. During this time, a couple may decide whether or not to marry.

__W__ **a.** Members of the community are invited to watch the couple promise to love each other **faithfully** with an **everlasting** love.

____ **b.** The man **surprises** the woman with flowers to show his **romantic** feelings for the first time.

____ **c.** The husband and wife disagree about the best way to **raise** their two sons.

____ **d.** Friends and relatives throw rice at the couple to make a wish for their **fertility**.

____ **e.** When a woman's boyfriend asks her to marry him, she is happy she won't have a **broken heart**.

____ **f.** The husband and wife hope that their marriage will **produce** healthy children.

____ **g.** A man and a woman are attracted to each other and choose to spend time together because of such **characteristics** as good looks, intelligence, and kindness. Little by little, each person discovers more about the other's **background**.

____ **h.** Important words are spoken by a person in a position of **leadership**.

____ **i.** The woman happily tells her mother that she is **pregnant**.

____ **j.** The man realizes that the woman will be an excellent **spouse**.

____ **k.** The husband and wife are **proud** of their children's achievements.

Ⓑ GRAMMAR: Simple Past and Past Progressive

1 *Read these sentences based on Frank Abagnale's story. Look at the boldfaced verbs. What is the difference between the verb forms? Notice the words in italics. How are the meanings of when and while different?*

- Frank Abagnale **was hiding** in France *when* a flight attendant **reported** him to the authorities.
- *When* he **met** the doctor who helped him, they **were** both **renting** apartments in the same community.
- *While* the FBI **was searching** for him, he **was enjoying** himself in California.

SIMPLE PAST AND PAST PROGRESSIVE	
1. Use the **simple past** tense to talk about actions, states, and situations in the past that take place at one point in time. The simple past tense of regular verbs is formed by adding **-d** or **-ed** to the base form of the verb.	He finally **passed** the law exam.
2. Use the **past progressive**, also called **past continuous**, to describe a continuous nonstop action that was in progress at a specific time in the past. Examples of specific time expressions include: **yesterday, last night, at that time**. The past progressive is formed like this: **be** (past) + **verb** + **-ing**.	**At that time,** he was **working** at a law firm.
3. Use the **past progressive** with the **simple past** tense to talk about an action that was interrupted by another action. Use the simple past tense for the interrupting action. Use **when** to introduce the simple past tense action.	He **was living** in France **when** a flight attendant **saw** him.
4. If you put the **when** clause first, you must put a **comma** at the end of the clause.	**When** the flight attendant **saw** him, he **was living** in France.
5. Use the **past progressive** with **while** to describe two actions in progress at the same time in the past. The **simple past** can also be used in the **while** clause without changing the meaning.	He **was enjoying** himself in California **while** the FBI **was searching** for him.
	He **was enjoying** himself in California **while** the FBI **searched** for him.

The **WRITING** section of each unit leads students through the writing process and presents a challenging and imaginative writing task that directs students to integrate the content, vocabulary, and grammar from the unit.

- Students practice a short **pre-writing strategy**, such as freewriting, clustering, brainstorming, interviewing, listing, making a chart or diagram, categorizing, or classifying.

- Then students organize their ideas and write, using a **specific structural or rhetorical pattern** that fits the subject at hand.

- Students then learn **revising techniques** within a sentence-level or paragraph-level activity to help them move towards **coherence and unity** in their writing.

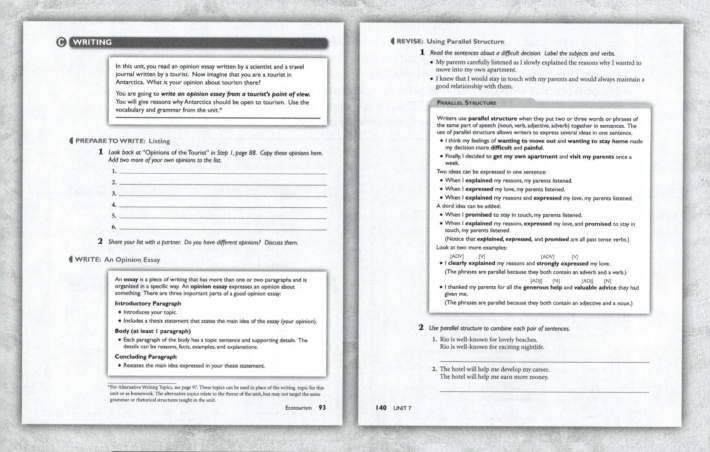

C WRITING

In this unit, you read an opinion essay written by a scientist and a travel journal written by a tourist. Now imagine that you are a tourist in Antarctica. What is your opinion about tourism there?

You are going to **write an opinion essay from a tourist's point of view.** You will give reasons why Antarctica should be open to tourism. Use the vocabulary and grammar from the unit.*

◀ PREPARE TO WRITE: Listing

1 Look back at "Opinions of the Tourist" in Step 1, page 88. Copy these opinions here. Add two more of your own opinions to the list.

1. _____
2. _____
3. _____
4. _____
5. _____
6. _____

2 Share your list with a partner. Do you have different opinions? Discuss them.

◀ WRITE: An Opinion Essay

An **essay** is a piece of writing that has more than one or two paragraphs and is organized in a specific way. An **opinion essay** expresses an opinion about something. There are three important parts of a good opinion essay:

Introductory Paragraph
- Introduces your topic.
- Includes a thesis statement that states the main idea of the essay (your opinion).

Body (at least 1 paragraph)
- Each paragraph of the body has a topic sentence and supporting details. The details can be reasons, facts, examples, and explanations.

Concluding Paragraph
- Restates the main idea expressed in your thesis statement.

*For Alternative Writing Topics, see page 97. These topics can be used in place of the writing topic for this unit or as homework. The alternative topics relate to the theme of the unit, but may not target the same grammar or rhetorical structures taught in the unit.

Ecotourism **93**

◀ REVISE: Using Parallel Structure

1 Read the sentences about a difficult decision. Label the subjects and verbs.
- My parents carefully listened as I slowly explained the reasons why I wanted to move into my own apartment.
- I knew that I would stay in touch with my parents and would always maintain a good relationship with them.

PARALLEL STRUCTURE

Writers use **parallel structure** when they put two or three words or phrases of the same part of speech (noun, verb, adjective, adverb) together in sentences. The use of parallel structure allows writers to express several ideas in one sentence.
- I think my feelings of **wanting to move out** and **wanting to stay home** made my decision more **difficult** and **painful**.
- Finally, I decided to **get my own apartment** and **visit my parents** once a week.

Two ideas can be expressed in one sentence:
- When I **explained** my reasons, my parents listened.
- When I **expressed** my love, my parents listened.
- When I **explained** my reasons and **expressed** my love, my parents listened.

A third idea can be added:
- When I **promised** to stay in touch, my parents listened.
- When I **explained** my reasons, **expressed** my love, and **promised** to stay in touch, my parents listened.

(Notice that **explained, expressed,** and **promised** are all past tense verbs.)

Look at two more examples:

    [ADV]   [V]   [ADV]   [V]
- I **clearly explained** my reasons and **strongly expressed** my love.
(The phrases are parallel because they both contain an adverb and a verb.)

             [ADJ] [N]   [ADJ]   [N]
- I thanked my parents for all the **generous help** and **valuable advice** they had given me.
(The phrases are parallel because they both contain an adjective and a noun.)

2 Use parallel structure to combine each pair of sentences.

1. Rio is well-known for lovely beaches.
Rio is well-known for exciting nightlife.

_____

2. The hotel will help me develop my career.
The hotel will help me earn more money.

_____

140 UNIT 7

In the final phase of the writing process, students **edit** their work with the help of a **checklist** that focuses on mechanics, completeness, enhancing style, and incorporating the vocabulary and grammar from the unit.

ALTERNATIVE WRITING TOPICS are provided at the end of the unit. They can be used as *alternatives* to the final writing task, or as *additional* assignments. RESEARCH TOPICS tied to the theme of the unit are organized in a special section at the back of the book.

MYNORTHSTARLAB

MyNorthStarLab supports students with **individualized instruction**, **feedback**, and **extra help**. A wide array of resources, including a flexible **gradebook**, helps teachers manage student progress.

The MyNorthStarLab **WELCOME** page **organizes assignments and grades**, and **facilitates communication** between students and teachers.

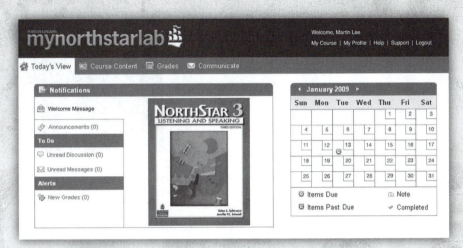

For each unit, MyNorthStarLab provides a **READINESS CHECK**.

➤ Activities **assess** student knowledge **before** beginning the unit and **follow up** with individualized instruction.

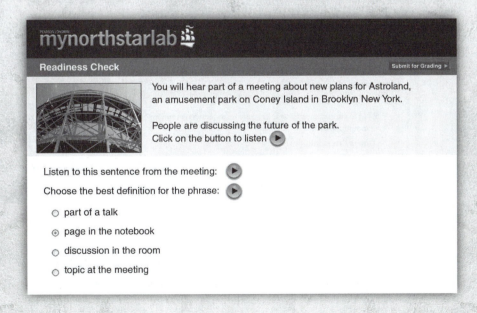

Student book material and **new** practice activities are available to students online.

➤ Students benefit from virtually unlimited **practice anywhere, anytime**.

Interaction with **Internet** and **video** materials will:

➤ Expand students' knowledge of the topic.

➤ Help students practice new vocabulary and grammar.

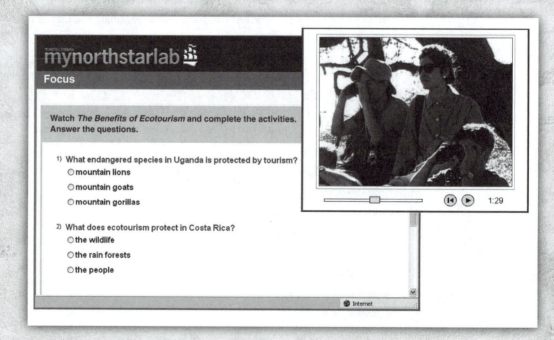

INTEGRATED SKILL ACTIVITIES in MyNorthStarLab challenge students to bring together the **language skills** and **critical thinking skills** that they have practiced throughout the unit.

The MyNorthStarLab **ASSESSMENT** tools allow instructors to customize and deliver achievement tests online.

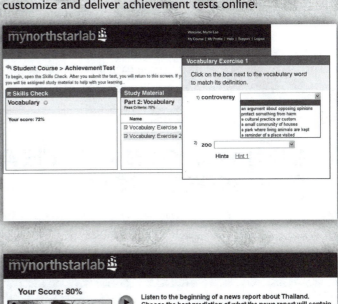

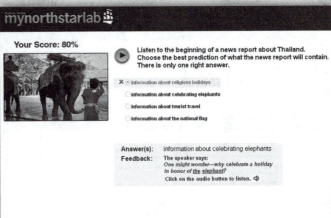

OVERVIEW OF THE TEACHER'S MANUAL AND ACHIEVEMENT TESTS

The **NorthStar Teacher's Manual** includes:

➤ Specific suggestions for teaching each unit

➤ Student Book Answer Key

➤ An alphabetized-by-unit word list of the key vocabulary items practiced in each unit

➤ Reproducible Achievement Tests with Answer Keys

UNIT-BY-UNIT TEACHING SUGGESTIONS

Unit-by-unit overview (scope and sequence), list of skills practiced in each section of the student book, suggested teaching times, teaching suggestions, suggestions on how to use *NorthStar* in secondary classes, Expansion/Homework activities, cross-references to the companion strand, techniques and instructions for using MyNorthStarLab

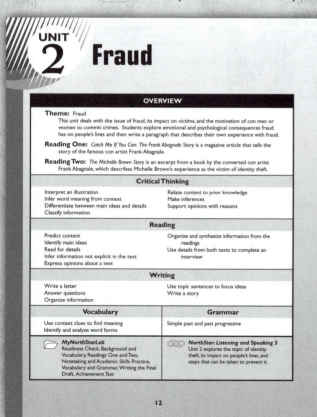

USING *NORTHSTAR* IN SECONDARY CLASSES

Each unit of the *Teacher's Manual* offers a set of strategies that provide opportunities for greater differentiation in a typical mixed classroom to meet the needs of multi-level secondary students. These strategies are equally beneficial in academic and adult classes. The scaffolded instruction enables teachers to facilitate student mastery of complex skills and ideas. Repeated exposure to concepts helps accelerate English language learning.

Reading/Listening Strategies give teachers additional support to guide students who have limited experience with basic reading/listening skills as they learn to explore and understand academic content. Suggestions are given to help students understand how to predict, determine main idea and supporting details, navigate and comprehend a text, monitor their understanding, and organize information.

Reaching All Students are activity suggestions for two levels of language proficiency, intended to assist less proficient students and challenge students with higher proficiencies. These are generally included in the Reading/Listening section to help teachers to modify reading/listening activities.

Critical Thinking suggestions focus on a hierarchy of questions using Bloom's taxonomy. These are designed specifically to scaffold questions to move students from knowledge-based questions to higher order thinking.

Vocabulary Expansion builds upon vocabulary introduced in each unit to help students further integrate vocabulary. The expansion activities are offered as word analyses or as vocabulary strategies to reinforce vocabulary skills and provide opportunities for review.

COURSE PLANNERS

Each unit contains approximately eight hours of classroom material, plus expansion, homework, and support material, including MyNorthStarLab. Teachers can customize the units by assigning some exercises for homework and/or eliminating others. To help teachers customize the units for their specific teaching situation, the unit-by-unit teaching suggestions in the *Teacher's Manual* include 1, 2, or 3 stars to indicate the relative importance of each section or exercise as follows:

✪✪✪ **Essential:** Predict, Background and Vocabulary, Reading One, Read for Main Ideas, Read for Details, Make Inferences, Express Opinions, Reading Two, Integrate Readings One and Two, Prepare to Write, Write, Revise, Edit

✪✪ **Recommended:** Share Information, Expand, Grammar

✪ **Optional:** Review, Create, Writing Topics, Research Topics

Class time available per unit	Sections to complete
8 hours or more	Essential (✪✪✪), Recommended (✪✪), Optional (✪)
6 hours	Essential (✪✪✪), Recommended (✪✪)
4 hours	Essential (✪✪✪) only

For more detailed, downloadable unit-by-unit course planners, visit www.mynorthstarlab.com or www.longman.com/northstar.

ACHIEVEMENT TESTS

The reproducible Achievement Tests allow teachers to evaluate students' progress and to identify areas where students might have problems developing their reading and writing skills. The Achievement Tests should be given upon completion of the corresponding unit.

Description

There are four parts for every test:

Parts 1 and **2** test students' receptive skills. Part 1 assesses students' mastery of reading comprehension. Part 2 assesses the knowledge of the vocabulary introduced in the unit. **Parts 3** and **4** test students' productive skills. Part 3 assesses students' knowledge of the grammar and style introduced in the unit. Part 4 is a writing test related to the content of the unit.

Administration

All parts of each test should be taken in class and students should not be allowed access to any *NorthStar* materials or to their dictionaries. Students should be able to complete Parts 1–3 within 30 minutes and Part 4 within 20 minutes.

Teachers can decide how to incorporate Part 4 (the writing task) into their testing situations. Some teachers will assign each writing task immediately after students complete Parts 1–3; others may decide to set aside another time to complete it.

Scoring the Parts

Parts 1–3: Individual test items are worth one point, for a maximum total of 30 points per test. A student's raw score can be obtained by adding together the number of correct items, or by subtracting the total number of incorrect items from 30. To convert the raw score to a percentage score, multiply it by 3.33.

Part 4: The writing tasks are evaluated holistically using scoring rubrics. The scale ranges from 0–5 and includes information from the reading and coherence/connectedness, paragraph development, structures and vocabulary from the unit, and errors.

Combining scores from Parts 1–3 and Part 4: To get a total Achievement Test score, multiply the writing test score by 2. Then, add the writing score to the score in Parts 1–3. Multiply this new score by 2.5 to get a percentage score.

Example 1	Example 2
Score on Test Parts 1–3 = 30	Score on Parts 1–3 = 23
Score on Part 4 = 5	Score on Part 4 = 3
Multiply 5 x 2	Multiply 3 x 2
Add 10 to 30	Add 6 to 23
Multiply 40 x 2.5	Multiply 29 by 2.5
Total score = 100%	Total score = 72.5%

Using the Scoring Rubrics

The *NorthStar Reading and Writing* rubrics are adapted from the integrated writing rubric of TOEFL iBT. Whereas the TOEFL iBT scoring rubric is intended to distinguish levels of English proficiency among candidates to colleges and universities, the *NorthStar* scoring rubrics are intended to show progress in students' writing at each of the five *NorthStar* levels. Therefore, *NorthStar* scoring bands make finer distinctions than TOEFL iBT's scoring band. In this way, students at each level will be able to both see improvement in their scores and receive high marks. The detailed scoring rubric is included in the Achievement Tests Answer Key.

Relationship between TOEFL iBT Rubric and *NorthStar 3* Integrated Writing Rubric		
TOEFL iBT	⟵⟶	*NorthStar 3*
3–4	⟵⟶	5
3	⟵⟶	4
3	⟵⟶	3
2	⟵⟶	2
1–2	⟵⟶	1
0–1	⟵⟶	0

OTHER NORTHSTAR COMPONENTS

EXAMVIEW

NorthStar ExamView is a stand-alone CD-ROM that allows teachers to **create and customize** their own *NorthStar* tests.

DVD

The *NorthStar* DVD has **engaging, authentic video clips**, including animation, documentaries, interviews, and biographies, that correspond to the themes in *NorthStar*. Each theme contains a three- to five-minute segment that can be used with either the *Reading and Writing* strand or the *Listening and Speaking* strand. The video clips can also be viewed in MyNorthStarLab.

COMPANION WEBSITE

The companion website, www.longman.com/northstar, includes resources for teachers, such as the **scope and sequence, correlations** to other Longman products and to state standards, and **podcasts** from the *NorthStar* authors and series editors.

UNIT 1

The World of Advertising

OVERVIEW

Theme: Advertising

This unit deals with legal, linguistic, and cultural challenges faced by global advertisers. Students familiarize themselves with various aspects of advertising, as well as issues and problems advertisers face in promoting their products globally. Students also describe and discuss their opinions about advertisements.

Reading One: *Advertising All over the World* is an article on global advertising.

Reading Two: *Changing World Markets* is an excerpt from a speech on changing markets in Russia and China.

Critical Thinking

Compare personal buying habits
Infer word meaning from context
Classify information

Identify and reevaluate assumptions
Connect themes between texts
Support opinions with reasons

Reading

Predict content
Identify main ideas
Read for details
Make inferences based on details from a text

Relate information in the text to life experiences
Link main ideas in Reading One to details in
     Reading Two

Writing

Write a TV commercial
Freewrite about an ad

Write a paragraph with a topic sentence,
    supporting details, and a concluding
    sentence
Write an opinion paragraph about an ad

Vocabulary	Grammar
Use context clues to find meaning Find and use synonyms and antonyms Use idiomatic expressions	Simple present and present progressive

MyNorthStarLab
Readiness Check, Background and
Vocabulary, Readings One and Two,
Notetaking and Academic Skills Practice,
Vocabulary and Grammar, Writing the
Final Draft, Achievement Test

NorthStar: Listening and Speaking 3
Unit 1 introduces the topic of advertising and
advertising techniques used to promote a
product.

FOCUS ON THE TOPIC

◀ SKILLS

Predict content; compare buying habits; infer meaning of new vocabulary from context.

✱✱✱ⓐ PREDICT

Suggested Time: 10 minutes

1. Have students look at the photograph on page 1. Ask them to identify the product. Then ask students if they have seen similar ads for this product in English or in another language.

2. Have students discuss question 1. Encourage detailed answers. Then have students answer question 2 and be prepared to explain why.

Expansion/Homework
Bring some unusual products (or photographs of unusual products) and have students try and describe them. Students can also share a product that is very popular in their home country but not easily found internationally.

 Link to NorthStar: Listening and Speaking 3
If students are also using the companion text, ask them to consider what kind of sound effects could be used in advertising this product on the radio.

✱✱ⓑ SHARE INFORMATION

Suggested Time: 20 minutes

1. Divide the class into groups of four (preferably of mixed language ability). Have students fill out the chart in **Exercise 1** individually and share their answers with the other students in the group.

2. Have students discuss the questions in **Exercise 2**.

3. Bring the class back together and invite students from each group to describe an advertisement they discussed. Elicit opinions on question 2 as well. Encourage diverging opinions.

Expansion/Homework
Assign the discussion question 1 in Exercise 2 for writing. Ask students to describe an ad that they often see or hear. Ask them to explain whether or not this ad makes them want to buy the product.

📁 Go to www.mynorthstarlab.com for *Background and Vocabulary*.

Suggested Time: 20 minutes

1. Have students read the definitions on the dictionary page. If they are having difficulty with certain words, provide sample sentences. Elicit sample sentences from students as well.

2. Have students complete the sentences. Go over the answers as a class.

📁 Go to www.mynorthstarlab.com for additional *Background and Vocabulary* practice.

②FOCUS ON READING

◀ SKILLS

Predict problems; identify main ideas and details; make inferences based on details from the text; express opinions about advertisements; read a transcript from a speech.

✱✱✱ **A** ▎ **READING ONE:** Advertising All over the World

📁 Go to www.mynorthstarlab.com to read and listen to *Advertising All over the World*.

Suggested Time: 25 minutes

Reading One is an article about the legal, linguistic, and cultural challenges advertisers face to promote products globally.

1. Have students work with a partner to write down two or three possible problems that global advertisers might face, such as language or misunderstandings. Ask students to consider whether or not products that are successful in their home countries would be successful in other countries.

2. Invite pairs to share their ideas with the rest of the class. Then have students read the article. The reading can be assigned as homework or lab work using MyNorthStarLab. You can also choose to play the recording of the reading and have students listen as they read.

READING STRATEGY: Previewing

I. Tell students that good readers usually take a few minutes to preview a selection as a first step to reading. It's helpful to know things like the length of a piece, the amount of time it will take to read it, and what the reading selection is about.

(continued on next page)

Remind them to always begin a reading selection by reading the title and subtitle, looking at illustrations, and reading charts and graphs. Then they should read the introduction (usually the first paragraph), the first sentence in each paragraph, and the conclusion (usually the last paragraph).

2. Have students preview the article and then share with a partner what they have learned. How much information did they get by previewing? Can they make a prediction as to the main idea and some of the details? Ask volunteers to share with the class and discuss what they think this reading selection is about.

✪✪✪ READ FOR MAIN IDEAS   Suggested Time: 15 minutes

Have students answer the questions individually. Encourage students to integrate the language of the questions into their answers. Go over the answers as a class. If there is any disagreement, ask students to point to the appropriate statements in the text that support the correct answers.

REACHING ALL STUDENTS: Read for Main Ideas	
• **Less Proficient:** To reduce reading demands, provide the paragraph number where the answer is located and have students work with a partner to answer.	• **More Proficient:** Suggest that students give specific evidence from the text to support their answers.

✪✪✪ READ FOR DETAILS   Suggested Time: 10 minutes

1. If necessary, have students read the article again. Then have them complete the exercise individually and then compare answers with a classmate's. In question 5, point out that *custom* refers to a specific behavior while *culture* is a broader concept that includes lifestyles, beliefs, and activities.

2. Go over the answers with the class.

Expansion/Homework
Initiate a discussion about customs. Ask students if there are particular customs in their home country for specific situations such as meeting new people, having a meal, etc.

✪✪✪ MAKE INFERENCES   Suggested Time: 15 minutes

1. Tell students that in this exercise they must decide on the best answer based on information from the text.

2. Read the campaign plans in items 1–5 as a whole class. Then have students complete the exercise individually and compare their answers with a partner's.

3. Go over the answers with the class. Encourage discussion.

Link to *NorthStar: Listening and Speaking 3*
If students are also using the companion text, have them list appeals that advertisers might use to promote the products in the campaign plans.

✪✪✪ EXPRESS OPINIONS   Suggested Time: 15 minutes

1. Go over the questions with the class. Allow students to form groups and discuss the questions for a few minutes.

2. Bring the class together and initiate a whole class discussion of all three questions. Monitor the discussion and be sure to let as many students as possible have the opportunity to speak. Encourage diverging opinions.

Expansion/Homework
The discussion questions can prompt a lively debate. In this case you may want to focus on only one or two of the questions in class, and assign one of the questions as a writing assignment for homework.

CRITICAL THINKING

Give students the following questions for discussion in small groups before discussing as a whole class:

1. What are the problems that advertisers have in a global market?

   Answer: Language, communication styles, differences in laws and customs, differences in likes and dislikes

2. How did advertisers solve the problem of language and communication styles?

   Answer: They wrote completely new ads for other countries.

3. How would you solve the problem of differences in laws and customs if you were an advertiser?

   Answers will vary, but might include hiring people who are knowledgeable about laws and customs of a country to create or review the ads. Students should support their answers with information from the text.

4. How would you solve the problem of different preferences among countries?

   Answers will vary, but might include market research to know the products that people in various countries like and advertising the items that are liked or accepted in the country. Students should support their answers with information from the text.

✪✪✪ B READING TWO: Changing World Markets

📁 Go to www.mynorthstarlab.com to read and listen to *Changing World Markets*.

Suggested Time: 15 minutes

Reading Two is an excerpt from a speech given by an advertising professional. The article expands the topic of global advertising, discussing how markets in Russia and China are changing.

1. Read the instructions for **Exercise 1** with the class and then discuss the questions as a whole class. Write key points and examples from the discussion on the board. Be aware that this discussion involves the issue of political freedom and can lead to heated debate. Be sure to moderate the discussion and keep it on topic.

2. Have students read the speech. You can also choose to play the recording of the reading and have students listen as they read.

3. Go over the questions in **Exercise 2** as a class. Ask students to cite specific information in the text to support their answers.

✪✪✪ C INTEGRATE READINGS ONE AND TWO

◖ SKILLS

Organize information from the readings and use this information to summarize the content.

STEP 1: Organize   **Suggested Time: 15 minutes**

1. Explain that students will need to link general ideas from Reading One with specific examples from Reading Two.

2. Have students complete the exercise. Go over the answers with the class.

STEP 2: Synthesize   **Suggested Time: 15 minutes**

1. Have students complete the exercise with a partner and then join another pair of students to compare answers.

2. Come together as a class and call on individual students to take turns reading the sentences in the paragraph. Encourage students to interject if they disagree with an answer.

📁 Go to www.mynorthstarlab.com for *Notetaking* and *Academic Skills Practice*.

FOCUS ON WRITING

A VOCABULARY

◖SKILLS

Review vocabulary from Readings One and Two by identifying synonyms; expand vocabulary by learning and using idiomatic expressions; identify and practice word forms; use new vocabulary creatively by writing a TV commercial.

✪ REVIEW   Suggested Time: 10 minutes

 Go to www.mynorthstarlab.com for *Review*.

1. Go over the instructions with the class. Explain to students that they must cross out the word that has a different meaning than the boldfaced word.

2. Have students complete the exercise individually. Then go over the answers as a class.

✪✪ EXPAND   Suggested Time: 15 minutes

1. Invite a student to read the excerpt from a description of a college course in advertising in **Exercise 1**. Then have students complete the matching activity. Go over the answers with the class.

2. Read the instructions for **Exercise 2** with the class. Explain to students that one word can have several forms—it can represent different parts of speech. Have students complete the exercise. Call on students to read their answers to the class.

3. If time allows, have students work out the forms of other words such as *succeed* or *describe*.

VOCABULARY EXPANSION: Personal Dictionary

Have students create a personal dictionary or vocabulary log to record unfamiliar words. Suggest that they organize it thematically (for example, *advertising*) and create boxes to record the information instead of simply writing definitions. Divide a rectangle into four sections. In the center, write the word; top left, write a synonym; top right, the definition; bottom left, a sentence; bottom right, draw an illustration.

✪ CREATE

Suggested Time: 30 minutes

1. Divide the class into small groups. Explain to students that you want them to write a TV commercial advertising a product of their choice. Elicit some product types from the class and point out the suggestions in the book. Explain that the TV commercial should not be longer than 60 seconds.

2. Have the groups complete the task. Move around the room and offer assistance where necessary. Remind students to use the vocabulary from the unit.

3. Invite each group to read or perform their commercial in front of the class. If appropriate, have the class vote for the best commercial.

Expansion/Homework
This activity could also be done individually as homework. In addition to TV commercials, you could also ask students to write an advertisement for radio or website.

 Link to NorthStar: Listening and Speaking 3
If students are also using the companion text, encourage them to use advertising techniques they learned in Unit 1 of the *Listening and Speaking* strand.

 Go to www.mynorthstarlab.com for additional *Vocabulary* practice.

✪✪ B GRAMMAR: Simple Present and Present Progressive

 Go to www.mynorthstarlab.com for *Grammar Chart* and *Exercise 2*.

◖ SKILLS

Distinguish between the simple present and present progressive tenses and their uses.

Suggested Time: 20 minutes

1. Have students compare the sentences in **Exercise 1**. Elicit the differences in the forms of the boldfaced verbs. Ask volunteers to explain the difference between the two forms.

2. Go over points 1–3 in the grammar chart with the class. Ask questions with adverbs of frequency to check understanding. Elicit non-action verbs that describe emotions, mental states, and situations. Then go over points 4 and 5.

3. Have the class complete **Exercise 2** individually. Go over the answers as a class and ask students to tell you which point in the chart their answer corresponds to.

4. Have students complete **Exercise 3** individually. Then review the answers with the class and ask students to cite the word or phrase that tells them which tense to use.

Expansion/Homework

For further practice, offer exercises from *Focus on Grammar 3*, 3rd Edition or Azar's *Fundamentals of English Grammar*, 3rd Edition. See the Grammar Book References on page 218 of the student book for specific units and chapters.

 Go to www.mynorthstarlab.com for additional *Grammar* practice.

C WRITING

If you wish to assign a different writing task than the one in this section, see page 18. The Alternative Writing Topics can also be assigned as additional writing topics for homework. The alternative topics relate to the theme of the unit, but may not target the same grammar or rhetorical structures taught in the unit.

◖ SKILLS

Freewrite about an ad; understand components of an opinion paragraph; distinguish between topic and detail sentences; integrate the concepts, vocabulary, grammar, and rhetorical structures from the unit to plan, develop, and write an opinion paragraph.

✪✪✪ PREPARE TO WRITE: Freewriting

Suggested Time: 10 minutes

1. Read the introduction to freewriting with the class and make sure students understand the concept of freewriting. Explain to students that as a culminating activity, they will write an opinion paragraph about an ad. Go over the information in the task box with the class.

2. Read the instructions for **Exercise 1** with the class. Have students choose an ad and freewrite about it for five minutes. Emphasize that they should write a description of the ad and express their opinions.

3. When they are finished, have students go over the instructions for **Exercise 2**. Tell students to read their freewriting and underline the descriptions. Then have them decide if the ad is effective and circle the reasons why or why not.

Expansion/Homework

Encourage students to keep an English language journal where they can freewrite on a regular basis. If they have access to the Internet, they can also create a blog. Stress that they can share their writing or choose to keep it private.

✪✪✪ WRITE: A Paragraph

Suggested Time: 30 minutes

1. Introduce the concept of an opinion essay. Explain that opinion essays are made up of paragraphs that contain information that supports the writer's opinion. Explain that in this unit, students are going to focus on writing an opinion paragraph.

2. Have students read the paragraph in **Exercise 1** and answer the questions. Read the explanation and have students compare their answers to the examples.

3. Ask students to complete **Exercise 2** individually. Then go over the answers with the class.

4. Have students complete **Exercise 3**. Then go over the paragraph with the whole class.

5. Read the instructions for **Exercise 4**. Have each student compose a topic sentence for their paragraph based on their freewriting. Check the topic sentences and go over the guidelines in **Exercise 5** for writing the rest of the paragraph. Then have the students write a first draft. You can also assign writing the first draft as homework.

✪✪✪ REVISE: Developing Paragraph Unity

Suggested Time: 20 minutes

1. Read the information about paragraph unity with the class. Then have students complete **Exercise 1**. Go over the answers with the class. Ask students to explain why the supporting detail sentence they chose does not work.

2. Have students complete **Exercise 2**, identifying the topic sentence of the paragraph and crossing out details that do not relate to it. Then go over the answers with the class.

3. Have students go over the instructions in **Exercise 3** and then analyze their own paragraphs, deleting sentences that do not support the topic sentences and replacing them with new sentences where appropriate.

Expansion/Homework
Bring in newspaper and magazine articles and have students identify topic sentences and supporting details in paragraphs.

✪✪✪ EDIT: Writing the Final Draft

Suggested Time: 20 minutes

Have students write the final draft of their paragraphs. Encourage students to use language and grammar from the unit. Make sure they go through the checklist before submitting their final drafts. Collect the paragraphs and correct them before the next class.

 Go to www.mynorthstarlab.com for *Writing the Final Draft.*

✪ ALTERNATIVE WRITING TOPICS

These topics give students an alternative opportunity to explore and write about issues related to the unit theme.

✪ RESEARCH TOPICS

Suggested Time: 25 minutes in class

1. Have students turn to page 211. Review the instructions for the activity with the class. Have students choose the advertisement that they think is most convincing and complete the worksheet.

2. Have students present and discuss the advertisements in small groups. Move around the room and offer assistance where necessary. Have the groups choose the advertisement that they think is most convincing.

3. Have the groups present the advertisement they chose to the whole class.

 Go to www.mynorthstarlab.com for *Student Writing Models, Integrated Task, Video Activity, Internet Activity*, and *Unit 1 Achievement Test.*

UNIT
2 Fraud

OVERVIEW

Theme: Fraud
This unit deals with the issue of fraud, its impact on victims, and the motivation of con men or women to commit crimes. Students explore emotional and psychological consequences fraud has on people's lives and then write a paragraph that describes their own experience with fraud.

Reading One: *Catch Me If You Can: The Frank Abagnale Story* is a magazine article that tells the story of the famous con artist Frank Abagnale.

Reading Two: *The Michelle Brown Story* is an excerpt from a book by the converted con artist Frank Abagnale, which describes Michelle Brown's experience as the victim of identity theft.

Critical Thinking

Interpret an illustration
Infer word meaning from context
Differentiate between main ideas and details
Classify information

Relate content to prior knowledge
Make inferences
Support opinions with reasons

Reading

Predict content
Identify main ideas
Read for details
Infer information not explicit in the text
Express opinions about a text

Organize and synthesize information from the readings
Use details from both texts to complete an interview

Writing

Write a letter
Answer questions
Organize information

Use topic sentences to focus ideas
Write a story

Vocabulary	Grammar
Use context clues to find meaning Identify and analyze word forms	Simple past and past progressive

MyNorthStarLab
Readiness Check, Background and Vocabulary, Readings One and Two, Notetaking and Academic Skills Practice, Vocabulary and Grammar, Writing the Final Draft, Achievement Test

 NorthStar: Listening and Speaking 3
Unit 2 explores the topic of identity theft, its impact on people's lives, and steps that can be taken to prevent it.

Go to www.mynorthstarlab.com for the MyNorthStarLab *Readiness Check*.

 ①FOCUS ON THE TOPIC

◖ SKILLS

Predict content; share prior knowledge about fraud; infer meaning of new vocabulary from context.

✪✪✪ Ⓐ PREDICT

Suggested Time: 10 minutes

1. Have students look at the illustration on page 19. Call on students to describe what is happening in the illustration.

2. Read the questions with the class and have students discuss them. Brainstorm different types of fraud with the class and draw a mind map on the board connecting students' ideas.

✪✪ Ⓑ SHARE INFORMATION

Suggested Time: 20 minutes

1. Go over the various types of fraud students brainstormed in the Predict task.

2. Divide the class into pairs. Have students interview each other, using the questions in the book. Invite students to share one answer with the class.

Expansion/Homework
Students may not have a lot of experience with fraud. If your students have Internet access, ask them to research famous frauds. They can report back either orally or write a short paragraph describing the fraud.

✪✪✪ Ⓒ BACKGROUND AND VOCABULARY

 Go to www.mynorthstarlab.com for *Background and Vocabulary*.

Suggested Time: 20 minutes

1. Read the instructions in **Exercise 1** with the class. Have students read the article, paying attention to the boldfaced words. Tell students to also underline any additional words and phrases that they aren't familiar with. When done, work with students to explain the meanings of the underlined words or phrases.

2. Have students complete **Exercise 2** in pairs or individually. Then review the answers with the class. Have students point out words or phrases in the article that helped them guess the correct meaning of the boldfaced words.

 Go to www.mynorthstarlab.com for additional *Background and Vocabulary* practice.

 # ②FOCUS ON READING

◖ SKILLS

Predict the content of the reading; identify main ideas and details; infer information not explicit in a text; express opinions about Frank Abagnale; read an excerpt from a book.

✱✱✱Ⓐ READING ONE: Catch Me If You Can: The Frank Abagnale Story

 Go to www.mynorthstarlab.com to read and listen to *Catch Me If You Can: The Frank Abagnale Story.*

Suggested Time: 25 minutes

In Reading Two, students read the story of Frank Abagnale, a famous con man who successfully impersonated many people.

1. Have students look at the poster from the movie *Catch Me If You Can.* Ask students if they have seen the movie. If so, ask them to tell the class what the movie is about.

2. Have students look at the list and predict three types of fraud that they think will be mentioned in the story. Call on students to read their predictions to the class. Affirm each prediction as a possibility. Then have students read the story. The reading can be assigned as homework or lab work using MyNorthStarLab. You can also choose to play the recording of the reading and have students listen as they read.

READING STRATEGY: Asking Questions

1. Tell students that turning the title and subtitles into questions will help to guide their reading of an informative text and determine what information is important. If a text has no subtitles, suggest that students turn the topic sentences into questions.

2. Have students begin by creating a 3-column chart and writing the title on the left side. Demonstrate how to turn the title into a question, which they will put in the center column of the chart. Tell students to assume that paragraphs 1 and 7 are the introduction and conclusion, so they should continue by writing the first

or second sentence in paragraphs 2–6. They will turn those sentences into questions, which they will put in the center of the chart. Then they should read for the answers to these questions, which they will write in the third column.

✪✪✪ READ FOR MAIN IDEAS   Suggested Time: 15 minutes

1. Have students work individually to put the events in the story in chronological order.

2. Draw an empty timeline on the board and elicit the sequence of events in the appropriate order. Complete the timeline on the board with the correct sequence of events.

Expansion/Homework
Timelines are very valuable tools to stimulate discussion in the past tense. Ask students to write a timeline listing the five most significant events in their lives and the dates they took place, and share this information with the class.

✪✪✪ READ FOR DETAILS   Suggested Time: 10 minutes

1. If necessary, have students read the story again. Then have students complete the exercise.

2. Go over the answers as a class and have students find the relevant passages in the story to support their answers if there are disagreements.

REACHING ALL STUDENTS: Read for Details	
• **Less Proficient:** Help students to locate the paragraph where answers might be found by first listing Frank's impersonations or circumstances by paragraph number (for example, paragraph 2—lawyer).	• **More Proficient:** Suggest that students locate two details that support or explain something about each of Frank's "lives."

✪✪✪ MAKE INFERENCES   Suggested Time: 15 minutes

1. Tell students that they will have to choose answers that they can conclude based on what they read in the article. Explain that the answers are not directly stated in the article, but can be understood based on other information in the text.

2. Have students complete the exercise individually and then discuss their answers with a classmate.

3. Go over the answers with the class and if there is disagreement, ask students to find passages in the story that support their answers.

❊❊❊ EXPRESS OPINIONS

Suggested Time: 15 minutes

Discuss all three questions with the class. Be sure to encourage a wide range of students to contribute to the discussion. Be sensitive to cultural differences in discussing respect and punishment. These are highly personal issues and students may be reluctant to share their thoughts openly with their classmates.

CRITICAL THINKING

Give students the following questions for discussion in small groups before discussing as a whole class:

1. Do you think Frank Abagnale's life was fun or stressful? Explain your answer.

   Answers will vary, but students should be able to explain their choice by using their own experience and information from the text.

2. In your opinion, what was his worst crime? Give reasons to support your answer.

   Answers will vary, but students should be able to support their opinion by using their own experience and information from the text.

3. Why do you think people believed him?

   Answers will vary, but students might eventually conclude that Frank was a good con man and people apparently trusted him.

4. What does the last paragraph tell you about Frank Abagnale's values? How are they different from his earlier values?

   Answer: He values being a family man and leading a simple life. The second part of the answer will vary, but might include his need for excitement and respect; his willingness to lie, cheat, and steal.

Expansion/Homework

You might want to play excerpts from the movie *Catch Me If You Can* in class and then discuss them with students.

❊❊❊ Ⓑ READING TWO: The Michelle Brown Story: Identity Theft

📁 Go to www.mynorthstarlab.com to read and listen to *The Michelle Brown Story: Identity Theft.*

Suggested Time: 20 minutes

In Reading Two, students read a third-person narrative about a woman's experience with identity theft and how it affected her life.

1. Explain to students that they are now going to read a story about fraud from the perspective of a victim. Ask students to identify the author of the story. Is this a surprise?

2. Have students read the passage in **Exercise 1** individually. Move around the room and explain any unfamiliar vocabulary. You can also choose to play the recording of the reading and have students listen as they read.

3. Have students complete **Exercise 2** individually. Go over the answers as a class.

 Link to *NorthStar: Listening and Speaking 3*

If students are also using the companion text, you can have them write a paragraph comparing Michelle Brown's story to Lily's story from Listening One in Unit 2 of the *Listening and Speaking* strand.

✪✪✪ C INTEGRATE READINGS ONE AND TWO

◀ SKILLS

Organize information from the readings in a chart; synthesize information from the readings to complete an interview.

STEP 1: Organize   Suggested Time: 10 minutes

1. Go over the instructions with the class. Be sure to point out that the chart has four quadrants, not just two columns. Elicit one answer from students and write it on the board.

2. Have students complete the exercise. Review the answers as a class. If there are disagreements, ask students to find the relevant passages in the readings to support their answers.

STEP 2: Synthesize   Suggested Time: 15 minutes

1. Divide the class into pairs and have students work together to complete the interview. Encourage them to use vocabulary from the unit, focusing on using their own phrasing to complete the sentences.

2. Invite a few pairs to read their completed interviews to the class.

Expansion/Homework
Have students continue the interview for homework. Each student can come up with two or three more questions to ask his or her partner.

 Go to www.mynorthstarlab.com for *Notetaking* and *Academic Skills Practice*.

③ FOCUS ON WRITING

Ⓐ VOCABULARY

◖ SKILLS

Review vocabulary from Readings One and Two; apply vocabulary learned in the unit to a new context—an online article; expand vocabulary by identifying and analyzing word forms and their relationships; use new vocabulary creatively to write a letter.

✪ REVIEW   Suggested Time: 10 minutes

 Go to www.mynorthstarlab.com for *Review*.

1. Go over the instructions with the class and then have students read the newspaper article individually and fill in the blanks with the correct words.

2. Go over the answers with the class.

Expansion/Homework
It can be fun to have students create their own cloze exercises. Students can take an article from a newspaper or from the Internet to use as a core text, or write their own text and gap it.

✪✪ EXPAND   Suggested Time: 15 minutes

1. Explain to students that one word can have several forms—it can have different parts of speech. Review the chart in **Exercise 1** with the class and complete the first item together. Point out that the word *duplicate* is a verb, and it can also be a noun and an adjective.

2. Have students complete the chart with the missing word forms. Encourage students to use a dictionary to help them find the correct words. Then go over the answers with the class.

3. Have students complete **Exercise 2**. Call on individual students to read their answers. Encourage other students to listen and correct their classmates where appropriate.

Expansion/Homework
Exercise 1 can also be done for homework. Point out to students that a chart like the one on page 30 is another way to organize their vocabulary notebook.

✪ CREATE   Suggested Time: 25 minutes

1. In this exercise, the focus is on retelling a series of events using the past tense in the form of a letter. Read the instructions with the class and make sure students understand the task. Tell them to use the new vocabulary from the unit.

2. Have students write their letters. Call on individual students to read their letters to the class.

Link to *NorthStar: Listening and Speaking 3*

If students are also using the companion text, you might want to list vocabulary items from Unit 2 of the *Listening and Speaking* strand and encourage students to use them in their letters.

 Go to www.mynorthstarlab.com for additional *Vocabulary* practice.

✹✹ B   GRAMMAR: Simple Past and Past Progressive

 Go to www.mynorthstarlab.com for *Grammar Chart* and *Exercise 2*.

◖ SKILLS

Understand, use, and contrast the simple past and past progressive tenses.

Suggested Time: 25 minutes

1. Analyze the example sentences in **Exercise 1** with the class. It is often useful to draw a timeline on the board to visually express the time an action took place. Use an *X* to indicate an event at a specific point in time and an arrow to indicate ongoing action in the past.

2. Review the grammar points in the chart. Invite individual students to read the explanations aloud to the class.

3. Have students look at the two cartoons. Elicit some ideas about the meaning of each cartoon. Go over the example in **Exercise 2** and have students complete the exercise individually. Review the answers with the class.

4. Go over the instructions for **Exercise 3** with the class. Have students write four sentences using *while* and *when*. If students can't think of a suspicious situation, allow them to write about another event from the past, as long as they use *while* and *when*.

5. Invite students to share their sentences with the class, or, if you have space, let them stand up and mingle, sharing their sentences with classmates as they walk around the classroom.

Expansion/Homework

(1) In pairs, have students choose a photograph from a magazine or the Internet and write a caption sentence using either *while* or *when.* Alternatively, students who are artistically inclined can draw their own cartoons. (2) For further practice, offer exercises from *Focus on Grammar 3,* 3rd Edition or Azar's *Fundamentals of English Grammar,* 3rd Edition. See the Grammar Book References on page 218 of the student book for specific units and chapters.

 Go to www.mynorthstarlab.com for additional *Grammar* practice.

C WRITING

If you wish to assign a different writing task than the one in this section, see page 37. The Alternative Writing Topics can also be assigned as additional writing topics for homework. The alternative topics relate to the theme of the unit, but may not target the same grammar or rhetorical structures taught in the unit.

◀ SKILLS

Answer key questions in a story; organize ideas chronologically; identify topic sentences, details, and conclusions; integrate the concepts, vocabulary, grammar, and rhetorical structures from the unit to develop and write a story.

✪✪✪ PREPARE TO WRITE: Answering Questions

Suggested Time: 10 minutes

1. Explain to students that as a culminating activity, they will write a story about an experience with fraud. Go over the information in the task box with the class.

2. Have students work individually to answer the questions. Tell students they will use these questions later on to write their story.

3. Call on a few students to read their answers.

Expansion/Homework

Remind students of notetaking techniques they have practiced and have them apply the same strategies to answering the questions.

❖❖❖ WRITE: A Story

Suggested Time: 30 minutes

1. Remind students of the writing task in Unit 1 (opinion paragraph). Elicit the components of a paragraph (topic sentence, supporting details). Explain that we use a similar structure in a story. Have students read the short introduction.

2. Have students read the paragraph in **Exercise 1** and answer the questions. Call on individual students to read the answers to the class. Then go over the explanation in the box with the class.

3. Call on individual students to read the questions in **Exercise 2** aloud. Have students discuss the questions as a class.

4. Have students read the instructions for **Exercise 3** and then refer them to their answers in Prepare to Write. Based on their answers, have students write a topic sentence for their story. Move around the room and offer assistance as necessary.

5. Once students have a workable topic sentence, have them move on to **Exercise 4** and write the first draft of their story. Explain to students that they should focus on content at this point and not worry about accuracy. You can also assign writing the first draft as homework.

❖❖❖ REVISE: Using a Topic Sentence to Focus Ideas

Suggested Time: 20 minutes

1. Read the introduction with the class. Be sure students understand the concept of a topic sentence before you move on to complete the exercises.

2. Have students read the paragraphs in **Exercise 1** and underline the topic sentences. Go over the answers with the class.

3. Next, have students complete **Exercise 2** by choosing the appropriate topic sentence for each paragraph. Invite students to share their choices with the class.

4. Review the instructions for **Exercise 3**. Have students work individually and share their new topic sentences with a classmate. Encourage students to peer correct. Invite students to write one topic sentence they created on the board. Have the class decide whether it is a clear topic sentence and encourage students to speak up and correct any language errors they may find.

5. Have students read the instructions in **Exercise 4** and then return to their first drafts and see if their topic sentences are clear and focused. Move around the room and offer assistance as necessary.

✪✪✪ EDIT: Writing the Final Draft

Suggested Time: 20 minutes

Have students write the final draft of their stories. Encourage them to use language and grammar from the unit. Make sure they go through the checklist before submitting their final drafts. Collect the stories and correct them before the next class.

 Go to www.mynorthstarlab.com for *Writing the Final Draft.*

✪ ALTERNATIVE WRITING TOPICS

These topics give students an alternative opportunity to explore and write about issues related to the unit theme.

✪ RESEARCH TOPICS

Suggested Time: 30 minutes in class

1. Have students turn to page 211. Review the instructions for the activity with the class. Tell students that they can also use a search engine to look for articles that provide information about recent cases of the type of fraud they have chosen to research.

2. Have students answer the questions about the fraud. Encourage them to write any additional information they found in the articles.

3. Have students present their findings in small groups. Have the groups prepare a report and present it to the class.

 Go to www.mynorthstarlab.com for *Student Writing Models, Integrated Task, Video Activity, Internet Activity,* and *Unit 2 Achievement Test.*

Going to Extremes: Sports and Obsession

OVERVIEW

Theme: Extreme sports

This unit examines the psychological and physical aspects of being obsessed with sports. It presents the theme from a perspective of a skateboarding champion, who found success through his obsession, and contrasts it with a story of a gymnast who became seriously ill as a result of her obsession with gymnastics. Students explore the topic and then write a newspaper report using the information from the unit.

Reading One: *An Interview with Tony Hawk* is a magazine interview, in which Tony Hawk talks about his obsession with skateboarding and how it had a positive effect on him while growing up.

Reading Two: *High School Star Hospitalized for Eating Disorder* is a newspaper article that describes a star gymnast's battle with anorexia nervosa.

Critical Thinking

Interpret photographs
Identify personal habits and attitudes
Infer word meaning from context
Differentiate between main ideas and details

Interpret character motivation
Use a Venn diagram to organize information
Brainstorm ideas

Reading

Predict content
Read for main ideas
Identify details
Infer information from context

Relate text to personal experiences
Organize and synthesize information from the readings

Writing

Use information from a Venn diagram to complete a paragraph
Write a descriptive paragraph

Identify components of a factual report
Write a factual report

Vocabulary	Grammar
Use context clues to find meaning Identify and use correct word forms	Ability: *Can, could, be able to*

📁 ***MyNorthStarLab*** Readiness Check, Background and Vocabulary, Readings One and Two, Notetaking and Academic Skills Practice, Vocabulary and Grammar, Writing the Final Draft, Achievement Test	***NorthStar: Listening and Speaking 3*** Unit 3 focuses on the topic of endurance sports and motivation of endurance athletes to practice their extreme sports.

①FOCUS ON THE TOPIC

◖ SKILLS

Predict content; express personal opinions about sports; infer meaning of new vocabulary from context.

✪✪✪Ⓐ PREDICT

Suggested Time: 10 minutes

1. Look at the photographs with the class. Call on individual students to identify the sports.

2. Discuss questions 2 and 3 with the class. Point to the title of the unit and have students discuss what it means. Encourage various interpretations of the title.

✪✪Ⓑ SHARE INFORMATION

Suggested Time: 20 minutes

1. Ask students to read the statements and mark them *A* for *agree* and *D* for *disagree.* Once students are finished, have them discuss their answers with a partner.

2. While students are discussing, write the statements on the board and to the right of the statements make two columns titled *agree* and *disagree.* Bring the class back together and ask for students' opinions on each question with a show of hands. Record the results in the appropriate column.

Expansion/Homework
For homework, ask students to interpret the chart you created together in class and write a short summary of the results. Compare the summaries and see if students all drew the same conclusions.

✪✪✪Ⓒ BACKGROUND AND VOCABULARY

📁 Go to www.mynorthstarlab.com for *Background and Vocabulary.*

Suggested Time: 20 minutes

1. Read aloud the definition of obsession. Discuss whether skateboarders and other extreme athletes ever do dangerous things. You might consider introducing the word *reckless* at this point to be even more precise.

2. Have students complete the exercise. Go over the answers as a class and provide some additional examples for the boldfaced words and phrases if the meaning is still not clear to all students.

 Go to www.mynorthstarlab.com for additional *Background and Vocabulary* practice.

②FOCUS ON READING

◖SKILLS

Predict content; read for main ideas and details; make inferences based on the text; express personal opinions about extreme sports and obsession; read a newspaper article.

❁❁❁A READING ONE: An Interview with Tony Hawk

 Go to www.mynorthstarlab.com to read and listen to *An Interview with Tony Hawk*.

Suggested Time: 20 minutes

Reading One is a magazine interview with Tony Hawk, in which he talks about his skateboarding obsession and the impact it has had on his life, especially when he was growing up.

1. Have students write their three questions individually. Invite several students to share their questions with the rest of the class. Affirm each question as a possibility.

2. Have students read the article. Move around the room and offer assistance with unfamiliar vocabulary. The reading can be assigned as homework or lab work using MyNorthStarLab. You can also choose to play the recording of the reading and have students listen as they read.

READING STRATEGY: Setting a Purpose for Reading

1. Tell students that setting a purpose for reading will help them to plan as they read and help them to remember what they have read.

2. Begin by brainstorming reasons why students might want to read something. Possible answers might include: to learn how to do something, to get information, to be entertained, to form an opinion about something, or to evaluate a piece of writing.

3. Have students read the titles for Readings One and Two in the Scope and Sequence of the student book and speculate on the purpose for reading each of those texts. Finally, have students work with a partner to determine a clear purpose for reading this text and have student volunteers share their ideas with the class.

✪✪✪ READ FOR MAIN IDEAS

Suggested Time: 10 minutes

1. Have students complete the exercise individually and compare their answers with a partner's.

2. Go over the answers as a class. If there is disagreement, ask students to find passages in the reading that support their answers.

REACHING ALL STUDENTS: Read for Main Ideas	
• **Less Proficient:** To provide practice in listening and fluency, have student pairs read each part in the interview aloud several times.	• **More Proficient:** Suggest that student pairs extend the imaginary interview to add more information about Tony Hawk.

✪✪✪ READ FOR DETAILS

Suggested Time: 15 minutes

1. If necessary, have students read the interview again. Then have students read the questions and write one-sentence answers individually. Then have them compare answers with a partner's.

2. Go over the answers with the class. If there is disagreement, have students refer back to the text to find passages that support their answers.

✪✪✪ MAKE INFERENCES

Suggested Time: 10 minutes

1. Tell students that inferences are conclusions that people draw based on what they know, read, or hear. Tell students that they will have to choose answers that they can conclude based on what they have read in the interview. Explain that the answers are not directly stated in the interview, but can be understood based on other information in the interview.

2. Have students complete the exercise individually and compare answers with a partner's.

3. Go over the answers with the whole class. If there is disagreement, challenge students to find passages in the text which support the inference.

✪✪✪ EXPRESS OPINIONS

Suggested Time: 10 minutes

Divide the class into pairs and have students discuss the questions. After a few minutes, put students in groups of four and continue the discussion. If time allows, invite a student from each group to share the key points of the group's discussion with the rest of the class.

CRITICAL THINKING

Give students the following questions for discussion in small groups before discussing as a whole class:

1. What do you know about skateboarding?

Answers will vary. You might ask student groups to list what they know on chart paper to share with the class. Encourage students to list an abundance of details.

2. What are the possible advantages and disadvantages of skateboarding as a career? Explain.

Answers will vary, but might include: limited opportunities, only the best will do well financially, potential for injury, danger vs. excitement, fun lifestyle, potential for fame, play as work.

3. What are the advantages and disadvantages of letting students design their own PE class?

Answers will vary, but advantages might include students being given daily school time to work on a potential career; it could encourage student creativity; students could work on a program that they love. Disadvantages might include lack of variety, students avoiding responsibility, or students engaging in dangerous activities.

4. If you could design a PE course for yourself, what would you design? Give advantages and disadvantages for taking your course.

Answers will vary, but the supporting reasons should be convincing.

 Link to *NorthStar: Listening and Speaking 3*

If students have completed or are working on Unit 3 of the *Listening and Speaking* strand, you might want to have them discuss the difference between motivation and obsession.

Expansion/Homework

You can have students discuss the question of whether obsession is the same as addiction. Students can write an opinion paragraph with their ideas, or research addiction and obsession and report back their findings to the class.

✪✪✪ Ⓑ **READING TWO: High School Star Hospitalized for Eating Disorder**

 Go to www.mynorthstarlab.com to read and listen to *High School Star Hospitalized for Eating Disorder*.

Suggested Time: 20 minutes

Reading Two is a newspaper article about a high school gymnast who was hospitalized with an eating disorder. Students confront an issue of obsession with sports that has a negative impact on a person's life.

1. Point to the picture of Nadia Comaneci on page 46 and discuss the requirement of the sport (agility, balance, strength, dedication). Next, have students read the title of the article and discuss how a gymnastics star might develop an eating disorder. Introduce the concept of anorexia and be sure students understand what it is before they begin reading. Be very careful with this subject as some of your students may have struggled with this problem.

2. Have students read the passage in **Exercise 1**. You can also choose to play the recording of the reading and have students listen as they read.

3. Have students complete **Exercise 2**. Go over the answers with the class.

✪✪✪ A INTEGRATE READINGS ONE AND TWO

◖ SKILLS

Organize information from the readings in a Venn diagram; use information from the diagram to synthesize the content from the readings in a paragraph.

STEP 1: Organize   Suggested Time: 15 minutes

1. Point to the Venn diagram on page 47. Go over the labels and make sure students understand that they should write characteristics the athletes have in common in the section where the circles overlap. Do one or two items with students to illustrate how to complete the exercise.

2. Have students complete the exercise.

3. While students are working, copy the diagram on the board. After students have completed their diagrams, call on volunteers to come to the board and complete the diagram.

STEP 2: Synthesize   Suggested Time: 15 minutes

1. Using the Venn diagrams they created, have pairs of students complete the paragraph in Step 2.

2. If time allows, invite pairs to read their paragraphs to the class. Encourage students to listen closely and interject if they disagree.

Link to *NorthStar: Listening and Speaking 3*

If students are also using the companion text, you might want to have them review the characteristics of endurance athletes and discuss which characteristics they think apply to Tony Hawk and Ashley Lindermann.

Go to www.mynorthstarlab.com for *Notetaking* and *Academic Skills Practice*.

3 FOCUS ON WRITING

A VOCABULARY

◀ SKILLS

Review vocabulary from Readings One and Two; identify and analyze word forms; write a descriptive paragraph using vocabulary and structures from the unit.

✪ REVIEW   Suggested Time: 15 minutes

📁 Go to www.mynorthstarlab.com for *Review*.

1. Have students look at the photograph of Gelsey Kirkland and discuss the skills and attributes required to be a ballet dancer. Then have students complete the exercise.

2. Go over the answers with the class.

✪✪ EXPAND   Suggested Time: 15 minutes

1. Remind students that many words have different forms—they can be different parts of speech. Tell students that in this exercise they will identify word forms for the words they have learned in this unit.

2. Have students complete the chart and compare their answers with a partner's. Encourage students to consult a dictionary if their answers differ.

Expansion/Homework
This activity can also be done for homework and the vocabulary can be added to students' vocabulary notebooks.

 Link to *NorthStar: Listening and Speaking 3*
If students are also using the companion text, you might want to repeat the exercise using the vocabulary from Unit 3 of the *Listening and Speaking* strand.

VOCABULARY EXPANSION: Word Forms

1. This activity can help students to recognize and apply suffixes that determine parts of speech. Remind students that one base word can assume many forms, depending on the addition of affixes.

2. Give students the following vocabulary words as a model: *obsess, obsessive, obsession; intense, intensive; controversy, controversial.* Help them identify the part of speech for each word. Ask students to provide other endings that change the form and function of the word (*-es, -ed, -ing*). Then have them work in small groups to identify other words and the suffixes that change their part of speech. Provide large chart paper so student groups can share their words.

✪ CREATE

Suggested Time: 25 minutes

1. Read the instructions with the class. Ask students to think of one achievement, hobby, or relationship that they would like to write about. Then have them write their paragraphs. Remind them to use five words from the box. Move around the room and offer assistance when necessary.

2. Call on individual students to read their paragraphs to the class.

Expansion/Homework
This activity can also be assigned for homework, with class time used to share paragraphs in small groups.

 Go to www.mynorthstarlab.com for additional *Vocabulary* practice.

✪✪ B GRAMMAR: Ability: *Can, Could, Be able to*

 Go to www.mynorthstarlab.com for *Grammar Chart* and *Exercise 2*.

◖ SKILLS

Understand the use of verbs that express ability.

Suggested Time: 20 minutes

1. Read the sentences in **Exercise 1** with the class. Ask students to tell you the meaning of the boldfaced words.

2. Next, invite students to read the points in the chart aloud. Answer any specific questions students may have.

3. Have students complete **Exercise 2** individually. Go over the answers as a class, inviting students to take turns reading one sentence at a time.

4. Read the instructions for **Exercise 3** with the class. Have students write five sentences about themselves using the target modals and related verbs. At least two statements should be untrue. Move around the room and provide assistance where necessary. Then have students exchange papers with a classmate and try and guess which statements are true and which are false.

Expansion/Homework
For further practice, offer exercises from *Focus on Grammar 3,* 3rd Edition or Azar's *Fundamentals of English Grammar,* 3rd Edition. See the Grammar Book References on page 218 of the student book for specific units and chapters.

 Go to www.mynorthstarlab.com for additional *Grammar* practice.

If you wish to assign a different writing task than the one in this section, see page 57. The Alternative Writing Topics can also be assigned as additional writing topics for homework. The alternative topics relate to the theme of the unit, but may not target the same grammar or rhetorical structures taught in the unit.

◀ SKILLS

Brainstorm ideas; identify key components of a factual report; organize information chronologically and according to the 5Ws; integrate the concepts, vocabulary, grammar, and rhetorical structures from the unit to write a factual paragraph.

✿✿✿ PREPARE TO WRITE: Group Brainstorming

Suggested Time: 10 minutes

1. Explain to students that as a culminating activity, they will write a factual report. Go over the information in the task box with the class.

2. Explain to students that brainstorming is an activity in which a group of people try to come up with as many ideas as possible. Tell the class to imagine they have the chance to interview Tony Hawk and ask him about how he landed the 900. Give students five minutes to write down as many questions as possible. Then invite students to share their questions with the class and write the questions on the board.

✿✿✿ WRITE: A Factual Report

Suggested Time: 30 minutes

1. Read the introduction and have students compare Reading One (an interview) and Reading Two (a newspaper article). Elicit the differences in style and purpose between the two texts. Then read the explanation of the 5Ws and offer clarification as needed. Pay special attention to the difference between an editorial (opinion) and a factual report.

2. Have students complete the first task in **Exercise 1**. Students can refer to the brainstorming questions on the board for ideas. Then have students complete the second task individually. Go over the answers with the class.

3. Have students plan their first drafts by completing the outline in **Exercise 2**. Walk around the room and offer assistance if necessary.

4. Go over the instructions for **Exercise 3**. Have students write the first draft of their paragraphs. If time allows, call on individual students to read their paragraphs to the class. You can also assign writing the first draft as homework.

Link to *NorthStar: Listening and Speaking 3*
If students are also using the companion text, you might want to give them an option of writing a factual report about Jay Batchen and his experience running the Marathon des Sables.

✪✪✪ REVISE: Considering Your Audience

Suggested Time: 20 minutes

1. Go over the information in the box and the examples with the class. Be sure they understand where to add additional information in a sentence.

2. Have students complete **Exercise 1**. Call on individual students to read their revised paragraphs to the class.

3. Go over the instructions in **Exercise 2**. Have students return to their drafts and underline any words or phrases in the text that require further explanation.

✪✪✪ EDIT: Writing the Final Draft

Suggested Time: 20 minutes

Have students write the final draft of their paragraphs. Encourage them to use language and grammar from the unit. Make sure they go through the checklist before submitting their final drafts. Collect the paragraphs and correct them before the next class.

 Go to www.mynorthstarlab.com for *Writing the Final Draft*.

✪ ALTERNATIVE WRITING TOPICS

These topics give students an alternative opportunity to explore and write about issues related to the unit theme.

✪ RESEARCH TOPICS

Suggested Time: 30 minutes in class

1. Have students turn to page 212. Review the instructions for the activity with the class. Emphasize that students should use the 5Ws they learned in the unit.

2. Help students think of individuals in their community that they can interview. Direct them to newspapers and websites they can use for more research. Then have students complete their reports at home.

3. Bring the class together and have students in groups present their factual reports. As a follow-up, ask the class which report was the most interesting.

 Go to www.mynorthstarlab.com for *Student Writing Models, Integrated Task, Video Activity, Internet Activity,* and *Unit 3 Achievement Test*.

UNIT 4

Speaking of Gender

Theme: Language

This unit focuses on the topic of language and gender. It explores the way in which gender affects language use. Students are introduced to the concept of gender and gender differences. They are also encouraged to discuss gender distinctions in language and differences between male and female speech, and write a contrast paragraph using information from the unit.

Reading One: *Different Ways of Talking* is a magazine article describing gender differences in the English language.

Reading Two: *Speaking of Gender* is an interview about gender-specific vocabulary.

Critical Thinking

Interpret a photograph
Assess gender typing
Infer word meaning from context
Differentiate between main ideas and details

Make inferences
Analyze gender influence in speech and behavior
Support personal opinions with examples from the text

Reading

Predict content
Read for main ideas
Locate details in the text
Infer information not explicit in the reading

Link readings to personal observations
Organize and synthesize information from the readings

Writing

Complete a paragraph using information from the readings
Write interview questions
Create a chart

Complete an outline
Use transitions of contrast
Write a contrast paragraph

Vocabulary

Use context clues to find meaning
Define words
Use idiomatic expressions

Grammar

Comparative adverbs

📁 *MyNorthStarLab*
Readiness Check, Background and Vocabulary, Readings One and Two, Notetaking and Academic Skills Practice, Vocabulary and Grammar, Writing the Final Draft, Achievement Test

🔗 *NorthStar: Listening and Speaking 3*
Unit 4 focuses on language and identity and how regional and social accents affect our perception of individuals.

 FOCUS ON THE TOPIC

◀ SKILLS

Predict content of the unit; identify and assess gender typing; share opinions about language; infer meaning of new vocabulary from context.

°°°A PREDICT

Suggested Time: 10 minutes

Have students look at the picture. Ask them if they think the baby is a girl or a boy and why. Then discuss the title of the unit with the class. Elicit students' ideas about the meaning of the word *gender*. If students don't know the meaning, explain that the term *gender* is usually used to refer to differences between men and women in speech, thinking, and behavior. Tell students that in Unit 4, they will look at gender and language.

°°B SHARE INFORMATION

Suggested Time: 15 minutes

1. Divide the class into small groups. Have the groups discuss the questions and write down the key points of their discussion.

2. Ask each group to share the key points of their discussion with the rest of the class. Note any cultural or gender differences in opinion, but be sure to keep the discussion calm and civil.

Expansion/Homework

Make a survey of class reactions to questions 1, 2, and 5. Ask students to write a brief paragraph summarizing the results of the survey and compare these results in a small group discussion.

°°°C BACKGROUND AND VOCABULARY

 Go to www.mynorthstarlab.com for *Background and Vocabulary*.

Suggested Time: 20 minutes

1. Read the instructions in **Exercise 1** with the class. Tell students to read the class description without worrying about new vocabulary items.

2. Have students read the class description again attempting to understand the boldfaced words.

3. Have students complete **Exercise 2** in pairs or individually. Then review the answers with the class. Have students point out words or phrases in the reading that helped them guess the correct meaning of the boldfaced words.

📁 Go to www.mynorthstarlab.com for additional *Background and Vocabulary* practice.

②FOCUS ON READING

◖ SKILLS

Predict the content of the reading; identify main ideas and details; infer information not explicit in a text; relate information in the reading to one's personal observations; read an interview.

❁❁❁ **A** **READING ONE: Different Ways of Talking**

📁 Go to www.mynorthstarlab.com to read and listen to *Different Ways of Talking*.

Suggested Time: 25 minutes

Reading One is an academic article in which the author discusses differences in behavior and language use by men and women, citing work by Deborah Tannen, a linguistics professor and bestselling author of books about language and gender.

1. Have students read the first paragraph of Reading One and write their answers to the questions. Then have them share their predictions in small groups.

2. Have the students read the article. Once they finish reading, have them check their predictions to see if they were correct. The reading can be assigned as homework or lab work using MyNorthStarLab. You can also choose to play the recording of the reading and have students listen as they read.

READING STRATEGY: Taking Notes with Graphic Organizers

1. Tell students they can improve their understanding of complex texts by taking notes as they read. For notetaking, helping students learn to choose an appropriate organizer will strengthen their ability to organize information.

2. For Reading One, show students three different organizers that perform the same function: a same-different chart, a Venn diagram, and a paper folded in two vertical halves. Model each graphic organizer using paragraphs one and two, and then have students choose the one they prefer to complete the rest of the paragraphs.

✪✪✪ READ FOR MAIN IDEAS

Suggested Time: 10 minutes

1. Have students scan the statements for any vocabulary they don't understand. Then have students work individually to identify the correct main ideas and rewrite the false ones.

2. Invite individual students to write their corrected false statements on the board. Encourage the class to correct any mistakes.

Expansion/Homework

This activity can be done for homework with the corrected false statements presented in class. Alternatively, you can ask students to write three additional false statements based on the reading and challenge the class to identify and correct them.

REACHING ALL STUDENTS: Read for Main Ideas	
• **Less Proficient:** Help students to comprehend the reading by asking them to record gender preferences in a simple two-column chart.	• **More Proficient:** Suggest that students chart gender rules and support each rule with examples from the text and their own knowledge and experience.

✪✪✪ READ FOR DETAILS

Suggested Time: 15 minutes

1. If necessary, have students read the article again. Then have students read the questions and complete the exercise individually. Then have students compare their answers with a partner's.

2. Go over the answers as a class. If there is disagreement, have students find the relevant passages in the article to support their answers.

✪✪✪ MAKE INFERENCES

Suggested Time: 15 minutes

1. Read the instructions with the class. Tell students that they will have to choose answers that they can conclude based on what they have read in the article. Then have students complete the exercise.

2. Go over the answers with the class and if there is disagreement, ask students to find passages in the article that support their opinion.

Expansion/Homework

This exercise is good practice for the TOEFL iBT. You may want to time the questions in order to simulate test conditions. Refer to *NorthStar Building Skills for the TOEFL iBT Intermediate* for more practice for the TOEFL iBT.

✪✪✪ EXPRESS OPINIONS

1. Divide the class into small groups. Have each group briefly discuss the questions.

2. Bring the class together and elicit ideas from each of the groups. Open up a whole class discussion. Be very careful when discussing gender roles. There are great differences among societies regarding gender roles and students can become offended by certain opinions.

CRITICAL THINKING

Give students the following questions for discussion in small groups before discussing as a whole class:

1. What are the differences in the way boys and girls play?

   Answer: They play different kinds of games, they play with different size groups, boys compete for leadership and play games with complicated rules, girls play in smaller groups with interest in sharing and playing fairly.

2. What are other ways that boys and girls interact differently?

   Answer: Girls are interested in gossip; boys gain status through their own abilities.

3. For what other reasons might boys/girls and men/women behave differently? Explain.

   Answers will vary, but students should explain and defend their responses. These might include size, strength, cultural expectations, education, and social, marital, or economic status.

4. What information in the article do you agree with and what do you disagree with?

   Answers will vary, but students should be prepared to support their opinions with clear reasons and examples.

Expansion/Homework

For homework, ask students to think about the following questions: *Do men and women learn differently? Should students be taught in single-gender classrooms?* Have students write a short paragraph sharing their opinion.

 Link to *NorthStar: Listening and Speaking 3*

If students are also using the companion text, you might want to bring the issue of dialect into the discussion by adding the following questions: *Do you think that men and women speak different dialects? Do they use different words or grammatical forms? Do you think the way that men and women speak affects their identity?*

✪✪✪ B READING TWO: Speaking of Gender

📁 Go to www.mynorthstarlab.com to read and listen to *Speaking of Gender*.

Suggested Time: 20 minutes

Reading Two is an interview with a professor of communications about gender-specific vocabulary in the English language. It gives students the opportunity to broaden the topic of gender differences in language.

1. Have students read the interview in **Exercise 1**. Move around the room and offer assistance with unknown vocabulary. You can also choose to play the recording of the reading and have students listen as they read.

2. Have students answer the questions in **Exercise 2** individually. Go over the answers as a class and encourage discussion.

Expansion/Homework
The reading could be done as homework, with class time used to discuss the questions.

✪✪✪ C INTEGRATE READINGS ONE AND TWO

◖ SKILLS

Organize information from the readings in a chart; synthesize information from the readings to complete a paragraph.

STEP 1: Organize   **Suggested Time: 10 minutes**

1. Go over the first example in the chart. Be sure students understand that they are looking for related examples of language use from Readings One and Two.

2. Have students complete the chart and compare answers with a partner's. Then call on individual students to read the answers to the class. Encourage other students to correct any mistakes.

STEP 2: Synthesize   **Suggested Time: 15 minutes**

1. Using the chart they completed in Step 1, have students complete the paragraph. Encourage students to use new vocabulary from the unit.

2. Invite students to read their paragraphs to the class. Encourage the rest of the class to listen closely and interject if they disagree.

📁 Go to www.mynorthstarlab.com for *Notetaking* and *Academic Skills Practice*.

③ FOCUS ON WRITING

A ❯ VOCABULARY

◖ SKILLS

Review vocabulary from Readings One and Two; apply vocabulary learned in the unit to a new context—a letter; expand vocabulary by identifying antonyms; use new vocabulary creatively to write interview questions.

✪ REVIEW   Suggested Time: 10 minutes

 Go to www.mynorthstarlab.com for *Review*.

1. Go over the vocabulary in the box and make sure students understand the meaning of each word. Read each word aloud and have students repeat chorally.

2. Have students read and then complete the letter. Go over the answers by having students take turns reading one sentence each.

✪✪ EXPAND   Suggested Time: 15 minutes

1. Have students read the paragraph silently. Elicit the meaning of the boldfaced words and phrases from students and offer explanations if necessary. Then have students complete the exercise.

2. Go over the answers with the class.

VOCABULARY EXPANSION: Sight Words

1. Tell students some words appear often in our reading. These words are called sight words. They are the most frequently used words in English. When students learn these words and can recognize them instantly, their reading comprehension will improve.

2. Provide students with a list of the hundred most common sight words and have them work in small groups to check off the words that appear in this interview. Then have them create a section in their personal dictionaries for sight words. Suggest that they select unfamiliar words from the list to add to their dictionary and include a simple sentence or drawing to help make the meaning of the word clear. To help students with these sentences, have student groups select several words to include on a word wall. Provide large index cards or sentence strips and allow time for groups to prepare a sentence and drawing for each word.

✪ CREATE

1. Read the instructions with the class. Make sure students understand that they must use at least one vocabulary word in each question. Have students write five questions using the words in the box.

2. Divide the class into pairs and have students interview each other using their partner's questions. Then have each pair summarize their interviews and share them with the class.

Expansion/Homework
(1) This activity can also be done for homework, with class time used to share and answer questions. (2) For more practice, students can expand their questions into written dialogue with Dr. Rockwell.

📁 Go to www.mynorthstarlab.com for additional *Vocabulary* practice.

✪✪ B GRAMMAR: Comparative Adverbs

📁 Go to www.mynorthstarlab.com for *Grammar Chart* and *Exercise 2*.

◖ SKILLS

Use comparative adverbs to compare actions.

Suggested Time: 15 minutes

1. Remind students that adverbs modify verbs. Then ask two students to read the conversation in **Exercise 1**. Ask students to explain the meaning of the boldfaced phrases from context.

2. Go over the explanations in the grammar chart with students. Make sure they understand the concepts before they move on to complete Exercise 2.

3. Have students complete **Exercise 2** individually. Go over the answers as a class.

Expansion/Homework
For further practice, offer exercises from *Focus on Grammar 3,* 3rd Edition or Azar's *Fundamentals of English Grammar,* 3rd Edition. See the Grammar Book References on page 218 of the student book for specific units and chapters.

Link to NorthStar: Listening and Speaking 3
If students are also using the companion text, have them turn to Exercise 2 in the Grammar section of the *Listening and Speaking* strand and use the comparative adverbs to describe how their English has improved in the past year.

📁 Go to www.mynorthstarlab.com for additional *Grammar* practice.

If you wish to assign a different writing task than the one in this section, see page 77. The Alternative Writing Topics can also be assigned as additional writing topics for homework. The alternative topics relate to the theme of the unit, but may not target the same grammar or rhetorical structures taught in the unit.

◀ SKILLS

Organize information in a chart; use transitions of contrast; integrate the concepts, vocabulary, grammar, and rhetorical structures from the unit to write a contrast paragraph.

✪✪✪ PREPARE TO WRITE: Charting

Suggested Time: 15 minutes

1. Divide the class into pairs and have them discuss the questions on page 73. Explain that they are going to write a contrast paragraph and these questions can help them plan what they want to write. If you have limited time, assign this exercise as homework and have students write some ideas to use in class.

2. Explain that one way to organize contrasting ideas is to create a chart. Go over the example in the Student Book and have students complete the list of differences. Remind them to use the comparative adverbs they learned in the Grammar section.

✪✪✪ WRITE: A Contrast Paragraph

Suggested Time: 30 minutes

1. Go over the explanation of a contrast paragraph with the class. You can refer back to the chart in Prepare to Write to help students visualize this structure.

2. Have students read the paragraph in **Exercise 1** and complete the outline with information and examples from the paragraph. Call on students to share their outlines with the class.

3. Go over the instructions for **Exercise 2** with students. Then have them write the first draft of their paragraph. Remind them to include a topic sentence and conclusion, as well as point-by-point contrasts. You can also assign writing the first draft as homework.

✪✪✪ REVISE: Using Transitions of Contrast

Suggested Time: 25 minutes

1. Call on a student to read the paragraph in **Exercise 1** to the class. Elicit the meaning of the boldfaced words and phrases. Go over the information about transitions of contrast with the class. Offer additional explanations and examples if necessary.

2. Have students complete **Exercise 2** by underlining the transitions in the paragraph on page 74. Then go over the answers with the class.

3. Next, have students complete **Exercise 3**. Tell them that some sentences might need to be edited to accommodate the transitions. Go over the answers with the class.

4. Have students complete **Exercise 4** and add transitions to their first drafts. Move around the room and offer assistance if necessary.

✪✪✪ EDIT: Writing the Final Draft

Suggested Time: 20 minutes

Have students write the final draft of their paragraphs. Encourage them to use language and grammar from the unit. Make sure they go through the checklist before submitting their final drafts. Collect the paragraphs and correct them before the next class.

 Go to www.mynorthstarlab.com for *Writing the Final Draft.*

✪ ALTERNATIVE WRITING TOPICS

These topics give students an alternative opportunity to explore and write about issues related to the unit theme.

✪ RESEARCH TOPICS

Suggested Time: 30 minutes in class

1. Have students turn to page 212. Review the instructions for the activity with the class. Direct students to TV programs they could watch. Go over the form and make sure that they understand each item.

2. Have students conduct their research. In class, have students work in small groups to discuss similarities and write a summary. Encourage students to show videoclips while they present their findings to the class.

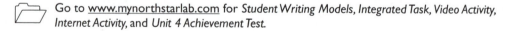 Go to www.mynorthstarlab.com for *Student Writing Models, Integrated Task, Video Activity, Internet Activity,* and *Unit 4 Achievement Test.*

UNIT 5 Ecotourism

OVERVIEW

Theme: Tourism
This unit focuses on the issue of how tourism might endanger the remote and fragile environments of the earth. Students explore the question of whether the interests of science and of tourism are incompatible, and write an opinion essay.

Reading One: *Tourists in a Fragile Land* is an opinion essay, in which a scientist explains his opposition to tourism in Antarctica and highlights the dangers of allowing visitors in that area.

Reading Two: *A Travel Journal* records the experiences of a tourist's exciting visit to Antarctica.

Critical Thinking

Use prior knowledge
Infer word meaning from context
Test assumptions about Antarctica
Differentiate between main ideas and details

Support opinions with reasons
Analyze author's arguments
Hypothesize another's point of view

Reading

Predict reasons
Identify main ideas
Identify inaccurate details
Make inferences based on details from a text

Relate the readings to personal opinions
Read a travel journal
Organize and synthesize information from the readings

Writing

Rewrite inaccurate statements
Write an opinion essay
Analyze the structure of an essay
Evaluate and write effective supporting details

Distinguish between facts, examples, and explanations
Organize ideas in an outline

Vocabulary

Use context clues to find meaning
Define words
Identify and use correct word forms
Find and use synonyms and antonyms

Grammar

Because and *even though*

MyNorthStarLab
Readiness Check, Background and Vocabulary, Readings One and Two, Notetaking and Academic Skills Practice, Vocabulary and Grammar, Writing the Final Draft, Achievement Test

NorthStar: Listening and Speaking 3
Unit 5 focuses on the positive and negative aspects of tourism and its impact on local culture and economy.

Go to www.mynorthstarlab.com for the MyNorthStarLab *Readiness Check*.

① FOCUS ON THE TOPIC

◖ SKILLS

Predict content of the unit; discuss travel experiences; infer meaning of new vocabulary from context.

✿✿✿ Ⓐ PREDICT

Suggested Time: 10 minutes

Have students look at the map. Call on students to identify Antarctica and describe its location. Ask students if they know of any other remote travel destinations. Write students' ideas on the board. Then discuss the questions as a class. Pay special attention to defining the term *ecotourism*.

✿✿ Ⓑ SHARE INFORMATION

Suggested Time: 20 minutes

1. Ask students to shut their eyes for a few seconds and visualize a place they have visited. Then invite individual students to share their destinations with the class.

2. Divide the class into small groups of three or four and have each group discuss the questions. Move around the room and ask additional questions. Provide help with vocabulary where necessary.

✿✿✿ Ⓒ BACKGROUND AND VOCABULARY

 Go to www.mynorthstarlab.com for *Background and Vocabulary*.

Suggested Time: 20 minutes

1. Ask students to read the vocabulary words and definitions in **Exercise 1**. If students are having difficulty with certain words, provide sample sentences. Elicit sample sentences from students as well.

2. Have students take the quiz in **Exercise 2** individually. Then go over the answers as a class. Ask students if any of the answers surprise them.

 Go to www.mynorthstarlab.com for additional *Background and Vocabulary* practice.

Expansion/Homework

To stimulate discussion, you could bring pictures of natural environments such as Costa Rica, Bali, and the Amazon. For homework, students could research nature preserves around the world and write a paragraph about them.

②FOCUS ON READING

❮ SKILLS

Predict reasons; identify main ideas and details; sequence ideas; identify inaccurate statements and rewrite them; make inferences based on details from the text; express opinions about traveling to Antarctica; read a travel journal.

✪✪✪ **A** **READING ONE: Tourists in a Fragile Land**

📁 Go to www.mynorthstarlab.com to read and listen to *Tourists in a Fragile Land.*

Suggested Time: 30 minutes

Reading One is an opinion essay written by a scientist who works in Antarctica. The author describes the negative impact tourists have on the area and the ways that tourism hurts scientific investigation. The style of the essay is somewhat formal.

1. Read the instructions with the class. Ask students what they think an opinion essay is and what ideas it might contain.

2. Have students read the first paragraph and predict reasons. Call on students to share their predictions with the class. Affirm each prediction as a possibility. Then have students read the rest of the essay. The reading can be assigned as homework or lab work using MyNorthStarLab. You can also choose to play the recording of the reading and have students listen as they read.

READING STRATEGY: Making Predictions

1. Remind students that good readers use their own knowledge, plus information in the text to help them decide what will happen next. Then, as they read, they confirm or change their predictions.

2. Have students practice this strategy with a think-pair-share. Before students respond to the instructions on page 82, tell them to use the information in the title and their own knowledge about Antarctica to help them think about how tourism might affect the environment. Next, have them read the first paragraph to help them think about how a scientist might feel about his work in Antarctica. Then, have students share predictions with a partner before sharing with the class.

✿✿✿ READ FOR MAIN IDEAS

1. Have students complete the ordering activity individually. Give students enough time to read the essay again if necessary to complete the task.

2. Go over the answers as a class. If there is any disagreement, ask students to point to the appropriate statements in the text that support the correct answers.

Expansion/Homework
This is a good opportunity to work with students on notetaking strategies. Most students have notetaking strategies they employ in their first language. Elicit a few strategies and introduce some of your own.

✿✿✿ READ FOR DETAILS

1. If necessary, have students read the essay again. Then divide the class into pairs (of mixed fluency if possible) and have students complete the outline in **Exercise 1**.

2. Go over the answers with the whole class. Ask individual students to read the details they completed. If time allows, ask students where the detail can be found in the text.

3. Go over the example sentence in **Exercise 2**. Then have students complete the exercise individually.

4. When finished, call on individual students to write their answers on the board. Invite the class to suggest corrections if there are errors in the sentences. If there is disagreement, ask the writer to point to the place in the text where the statement can be found. Allow paraphrases as long as the content is factually correct.

Expansion/Homework
The Read for Main Ideas and/or Read for Details activities could be assigned for homework. The answers could then be discussed in class, first in pairs and then as a whole class.

✿✿✿ MAKE INFERENCES

1. Draw a horizontal line on the board. On the left end of the line write the word *definitely*. On the right end write the word *never*. Underneath the line write the words *likely, unlikely,* and *probably*.

2. Invite a student to the board and ask him or her to place the three words in the appropriate place on the line. Ask the class if they agree. Make changes if necessary.

3. Explain that in the following exercise students must decide how likely or unlikely a statement is based on information from the text.

4. Have students complete the exercise. Then go over the answers as a class. Encourage discussion.

REACHING ALL STUDENTS: Make Inferences

- **Less Proficient:** To help students find the paragraph where the inferential information is located, show them how important words are repeated.

- **More Proficient:** Suggest that students write a short explanation for each inferential answer in their own words, using information from the text and from their own knowledge.

❁❁❁ EXPRESS OPINIONS

Suggested Time: 15 minutes

1. Tell students that it is now their turn to express their own opinions about the topic of Antarctica.

2. Divide the class into small groups and assign each group one of the three questions to discuss.

3. Have each group choose a group member to report on their discussions with the rest of the class. Alternatively, if you have a large class you can assign the three questions to groups in multiples of three. Then you can combine these groups and have them summarize their discussions to each other rather than to the whole class.

Expansion/Homework

You can ask students to write a short opinion essay on one of the questions for homework.

CRITICAL THINKING

Give students the following questions for discussion in small groups before discussing as a whole class:

1. What are the reasons the scientist gives for closing Antarctica to tourists?

   Answer: We should preserve Antarctica for scientific research; tourists take scientists away from their work; tourists damage the environment; there is no government to protect Antarctica.

2. Give examples of how tourism can harm Antarctica.

   Answer: Trash on beaches, damage to plants, damage to penguin eggs, oil spills

3. In your opinion, are the scientist's reasons strong enough to close the continent to tourists? Support your opinion with good reasons of your own.

   Answers will vary. Ensure that students support their opinions.

4. Choose one of the scientist's arguments against tourism and determine a way to solve it without closing the continent to tourists.

   Answers will vary. Students should be encouraged to be creative in addressing this issue.

✪✪✪ B | READING TWO: A Travel Journal

 Go to www.mynorthstarlab.com to read and listen to *A Travel Journal.*

Suggested Time: 20 minutes

Reading Two is a diary, in which students read an informal account of a tourist's trip to Antarctica. The purpose of this reading is to look at tourism to Antarctica from a personal perspective.

1. Ask students if they keep a journal or diary. Ask them what kind of information they include in their journals or might be included in a journal. Can they think of any famous journals or diaries?

2. Explain that many travelers have kept diaries throughout history. Give an example that you know and they may know, for example, Charles Darwin, Captain Cook, Lewis and Clarke. Tell them they are going to read a diary of a traveler to Antarctica.

3. Have students read the text in **Exercise 1** individually. Move around the room and help with any difficult vocabulary. You can also choose to play the recording of the reading and have students listen as they read.

4. Go over the questions in **Exercise 2** as a class. Ask students where in the diary the answers can be found.

Expansion/Homework

This might be a good opportunity to encourage students to begin keeping their own journals, where they can reflect on what they learn in class.

Link to *NorthStar: Listening and Speaking 3*

If students are also using the companion text, have them use the comprehension questions from Reading Two to discuss the travel blog in Unit 5 of the *Listening and Speaking* strand.

✪✪✪ C | INTEGRATE READINGS ONE AND TWO

◖ SKILLS

Organize information from the readings in a chart; synthesize information from the readings to complete and role-play a conversation.

STEP 1: Organize   **Suggested Time: 15 minutes**

1. Point to the chart and go through the example with the class. Explain that students must complete the chart with information from both readings.

2. Divide the class into pairs and have students complete the task. Then match two pairs of students and have them compare their answers.

3. Go over the answers with the entire class.

STEP 2: Synthesize

Suggested Time: 20 minutes

1. Keep students together with their partners from Step 1.

2. Explain that they are going to create a role play based on the information in the chart they completed in Step 1.

3. Tell students that they should make the conversation as natural as possible. Move around the room and offer assistance where necessary.

4. When all students are finished, invite a few pairs to come up and act out their conversations. Challenge students to continue the conversation beyond the lines on the page.

 Go to www.mynorthstarlab.com for *Notetaking* and *Academic Skills Practice*.

 ③FOCUS ON WRITING

Ⓐ VOCABULARY

◖ SKILLS

Review vocabulary from Readings One and Two; expand vocabulary by identifying and analyzing word types and their relationships; complete analogies; create sentences using new vocabulary.

✪ REVIEW

Suggested Time: 15 minutes

 Go to www.mynorthstarlab.com for *Review*.

1. Go over the example with the class. Explain that some adjective-noun combinations are obvious while others are more subtle and hard to identify. Tell students that they should be sure that their choices are supported by the texts.

2. Have students begin working individually. After a few minutes, ask students to form small groups and pool their ideas. Have students correct each other if there are incorrect combinations.

3. Bring the class together and write the combinations on the board. If there are still mistakes, see if the class can identify them, otherwise point them out and elicit legitimate combinations.

Expansion/Homework

In addition to creating individual combinations, assign pairs of students one of the nouns and ask them to make a word web with as many adjectives they can think of for each word.

Link to *NorthStar: Listening and Speaking 3*
If students are also using the companion text, you may want to repeat the exercise for homework using vocabulary from Unit 5 of the *Listening and Speaking* strand.

✪✪ EXPAND

Suggested Time: 20 minutes

1. Go over the information in the chart with the class. Elicit some additional examples from individual students.

2. Do item 1 with the whole class. Make sure students understand that they must identify the relationship between the words and choose the correct word to complete the equation. Have students complete the exercise on their own and then compare their answers with a partner's.

3. Bring the class together and ask individual students to share their answers.

VOCABULARY EXPANSION: Suffixes

1. Have students write the root/base word and the suffix for these vocabulary words: *coastal* (*coast* + *al*), *tourist* (*tour* + *ist*), *scenic* (*scene* + *ic*).

2. Have students brainstorm examples of other words that use these suffixes and then check the meaning of the suffixes in a dictionary.

   For example,
   -al   parental, viral, bacterial, sentimental, comical, educational
   -ist biologist, dentist, novelist, pianist, scientist, typist, violinist
   -ic   academic, comic, economic, electric, geographic

3. Students can then add the suffixes to the section designated in their vocabulary notebooks.

✪ CREATE

Suggested Time: 20 minutes

1. Explain to students that they will write sentences about a place of natural beauty. Tell them that if they have never visited such a place personally, they can write about a place they may have seen in pictures or movies, or read about in books.

2. Have students write their sentences individually and then exchange papers with a partner who will check the sentences for errors. Consider introducing an error marking system to the students. When students correct each other, make sure they use the system.

3. Call on individual students to read their sentences to the class.

Expansion/Homework

Ask students to find a landscape photograph on the Internet, in a book, or a magazine. Then have students write a short paragraph about the picture using as much target vocabulary from the unit as possible. Alternatively, you can select the pictures and hand them out to students.

 Go to www.mynorthstarlab.com for additional *Vocabulary* practice.

✪✪ B GRAMMAR: *Because* and *Even though*

 Go to www.mynorthstarlab.com for *Grammar Chart* and *Exercise 2*.

◖ SKILLS

Learn the difference between *because* and *even though* and write compound sentences using both phrases.

Suggested Time: 20 minutes

1. Read the sentences in **Exercise 1** with the class. See if students can paraphrase them and retain the same meaning.

2. Go over the chart with the class. Ask individual students to read the explanations and the examples.

3. Point out that sentences including *because* answer questions beginning with *why*. Ask a few *why* questions and elicit answers containing *because*.

4. Explain to students that when *even though* is used in a sentence, it often implies a hidden motive or reason which is not explicitly stated. Read the examples in the chart and the sample sentence in Exercise 2, and ask students to speculate about the reason or motive.

5. Have students complete **Exercise 2**. Go over the answers as a class. Pay special attention to the appropriate placement of commas.

6. Next, have students complete **Exercise 3** and share their answers with a partner. Invite individual students to read their answers to the class.

Expansion/Homework

For further practice, offer exercises from *Focus on Grammar 3*, 3rd Edition or Azar's *Fundamentals of English Grammar*, 3rd Edition. See the Grammar Book References on page 218 of the student book for specific units and chapters.

 Go to www.mynorthstarlab.com for additional *Grammar* practice.

If you wish to assign a different writing task than the one in this section, see page 97. The Alternative Writing Topics can also be assigned as additional writing topics for homework. The alternative topics relate to the theme of the unit but may not target the same grammar or rhetorical structures taught in the unit.

◀ SKILLS

Use listing as a pre-writing technique; understand the components of an opinion essay; identify thesis sentences, topic sentences, and details; integrate the concepts, vocabulary, grammar, and rhetorical structures from the unit to write an opinion essay.

✲✲✲ PREPARE TO WRITE: Listing

Suggested Time: 10 minutes

1. Explain to students that as a culminating activity, they will write an opinion essay. Go over the information in the task box with the class.

2. Give students a few minutes to complete the list of opinions in **Exercise 1**. Then have them share their opinions with a partner.

3. Match two pairs and have students share their opinions in groups of four (**Exercise 2**).

4. Ask one student from each group to summarize the opinions in each group for the entire class. Write each original opinion on the board.

✲✲✲ WRITE: An Opinion Essay

Suggested Time: 35 minutes

1. Ask students if they can remember writing an opinion essay in their native language. Elicit the structure of an opinion essay and write the key components on the board. Then have students read the information in the box. Explain further if necessary.

2. Have students complete **Exercise 1**. Go over the answers as a class. Pay special attention to the distinction between a thesis statement and a topic sentence.

3. Read the instructions for **Exercise 2** with the class. Make sure students understand the objectives of the exercise. Then have them complete the exercise. Move around the room and provide assistance where necessary. This is a difficult task for many students. Point to any errors you may find, but encourage students to make corrections themselves.

4. Go over the instructions for **Exercise 3** with the class. Have students write the first draft of their essays. Don't allow them to use a dictionary while writing as this will slow down the process. The core vocabulary students need is all available in the unit. You can also assign writing the first draft as homework.

Link to *NorthStar: Listening and Speaking 3*

If students are also using the companion text, you might want to have them write an opinion essay on tourism and culture using examples from Unit 5 of the *Listening and Speaking* strand.

❂❂❂ REVISE: Choosing Effective Supporting Details

Suggested Time: 20 minutes

1. Have one student read the explanation to the class. Explain to students that effective supporting details are essential to a well-written essay.

2. Point to the instructions for **Exercise 1**. Tell students they will read an essay that does not have effective supporting details. Have students read the essay and think what makes the details weak.

3. Have students complete **Exercise 2**. Call on individual students and ask them to identify the type of supporting detail found in each new section. Then go over the instructions for **Exercise 3**. Make sure students are clear about the differences between facts, examples, and explanations. Elicit some examples of each from the readings in the unit.

4. Have students read the instructions for **Exercise 4** and then review their own drafts. Move around the room and make comments where appropriate. Don't rewrite or offer specific alternatives to students. Have them think it through. Alternatively, you can have students exchange essays and peer correct them.

❂❂❂ EDIT: Writing the Final Draft

Suggested Time: 20 minutes

Have students write the final draft of their essays. Encourage them to use language and grammar from the unit. Make sure they go through the checklist before submitting their final drafts. Collect the essays and correct them before the next class.

 Go to www.mynorthstarlab.com for *Writing the Final Draft.*

✪ ALTERNATIVE WRITING TOPICS

These topics give students an alternative opportunity to explore and write about issues related to the unit theme.

✪ RESEARCH TOPICS

Suggested Time: 25 minutes in class

1. Have students turn to page 213. Review the instructions for the activity with the class. Tell students to use a search engine to look for organizations that are working to protect the Arctic environment.

2. Have students write their letters to the organization of their choice. You might want to post a few example letters on a class bulletin board or web page. Encourage students to ask additional questions in their letters.

3. Have students present their letters to the class. As they receive answers to their letters, ask students to share them with the class.

 Go to www.mynorthstarlab.com for *Student Writing Models, Integrated Task, Video Activity, Internet Activity,* and *Unit 5 Achievement Test.*

UNIT 6

The Metamorphosis

<table>
<tr><td colspan="2" align="center">OVERVIEW</td></tr>
</table>

Theme: Storytelling

This unit examines our attitudes towards insects through an abridged version of Kafka's "The Metamorphosis," a story in which a man wakes up to discover he has become a cockroach. Students read the story and make connections between the author's life and the main character in the story. They are also introduced to basic literary analysis. Finally, students write a story using the information from the unit.

Reading One: *The Metamorphosis* is an abridged version of Kafka's story.

Reading Two: *Ungeziefer* is a critic's interpretation of Kafka's "The Metamorphosis."

Critical Thinking

Recognize personal assumptions
Infer word meaning from context
Reflect on attitudes towards insects
Infer ideas not explicit in a text

Examine symbols and imagery in a text
Classify information
Interpret emotions

Reading

Make predictions
Recognize main ideas
Paraphrase details

Interpret a literary text
Support answers with information from the text
Connect generalizations to specific passages

Writing

Write an interview
Write a descriptive paragraph
Answer *wh-* questions

Add details to a story
Write a story with a moral

Vocabulary	Grammar
Use context clues to find meaning Complete a crossword puzzle Find and use synonyms	Infinitives of purpose

📁 **MyNorthStarLab** Readiness Check, Background and Vocabulary, Readings One and Two, Notetaking and Academic Skills Practice, Vocabulary and Grammar, Writing the Final Draft, Achievement Test	◯◯ **NorthStar: Listening and Speaking 3** Unit 6 explores the art of storytelling and techniques storytellers use.

Go to www.mynorthstarlab.com for the MyNorthStarLab *Readiness Check*.

1 FOCUS ON THE TOPIC

◀ SKILLS

Reflect on attitudes towards insects and brainstorm descriptive vocabulary; predict the content of the unit; share experiences with and knowledge of insects; infer meaning of new vocabulary from context.

✱✱✱ A PREDICT

Suggested Time: 10 minutes

1. Have students look at the photograph of the cockroach. In small groups, have students brainstorm two lists: adjectives that describe the cockroach and adjectives that describe their feelings about cockroaches. Ask students to share their lists as you write them on the board.

2. Call on students to share their predictions about the content of the unit. Affirm each prediction as a possibility.

✱✱ B SHARE INFORMATION

Suggested Time: 20 minutes

Divide the class into small groups and have students discuss the questions. Encourage students to share any interesting anecdotes or information about insects. Move around the room and offer assistance with vocabulary if needed. Then invite one student from each group to share their ideas with the class.

✱✱✱ C BACKGROUND AND VOCABULARY

Go to www.mynorthstarlab.com for *Background and Vocabulary*.

Suggested Time: 25 minutes

1. Focus students on the photograph of Franz Kafka. See if any students recognize the author. If so, elicit any facts they might know.

2. Tell students they will read a short biography of Franz Kafka. Tell them to read the text in **Exercise 1** without worrying about new vocabulary items. Then have them read the text again attempting to understand the boldfaced words.

3. Have students complete **Exercise 2** in pairs or individually. Then review the answers with the class. Explain any other unfamiliar vocabulary.

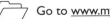 Go to www.mynorthstarlab.com for additional *Background and Vocabulary* practice.

 # FOCUS ON READING

◖ SKILLS

Predict and interpret the content of a story; correct main ideas; paraphrase details; infer ideas not explicit in the text; express opinions and interpret a literary text.

✪✪✪ A READING ONE: The Metamorphosis

 Go to www.mynorthstarlab.com to read and listen to *The Metamorphosis*.

Suggested Time: 25 minutes

Reading One is an abridged version of "The Metamorphosis" by Franz Kafka.

1. Remind students of the photograph of the cockroach and the word *metamorphosis*. With these two ideas in mind, have students read the paragraph and answer the questions that follow.

2. Call on individual students to share their ideas with the rest of the class. Encourage alternative interpretations.

3. Have students read the rest of the story. The reading can be assigned as homework or lab work using MyNorthStarLab. You can also choose to play the recording of the reading and have students listen as they read.

REACHING ALL STUDENTS: Reacting to the Reading

- **Less Proficient:** Help students to answer the questions by allowing them to discuss the answers in small groups before they write.

- **More Proficient:** Suggest that students choose one of the questions for elaboration in a short paragraph. They should include evidence from the story to support their responses.

✪✪✪ READ FOR MAIN IDEAS   **Suggested Time: 15 minutes**

1. Have students scan the false statements for any vocabulary they don't understand. Then have students work individually to correct the main ideas.

2. Call on students to share their answers. Encourage them to use their own words in their answers.

Expansion/Homework

Choose a short story for students to read and have them write at least five false main idea sentences for their classmates to rewrite.

READING STRATEGY: Narrative and Informative Texts

1. Help students to distinguish between narrative and informative texts by showing them an example of each. Explain that we read each of these differently because we are reading for different reasons. When we read a narrative text, we want to know about the characters and what happens to them. When we read an informative text, we are reading for information.

2. Ask students to identify the type of text in Reading One and Reading Two. Once we are clear that Reading One is a story, or narrative, show students how to create a story map or chart to record story elements (character, setting, problem, events, and resolution). For Reading Two, students might create a simple outline of points in response to the questions in paragraph 2.

✪✪✪ READ FOR DETAILS   Suggested Time: 15 minutes

1. If necessary, have students read the story again. Then review the concept of paraphrasing and go over the example with the class.

2. Have students find sentences in the text with the same meaning as the paraphrases in the exercise. Then call on students to read their sentences to the class. If there is disagreement, ask students to find the relevant passages in the story that support their answers.

✪✪✪ MAKE INFERENCES   Suggested Time: 15 minutes

1. Remind students that inferences are conclusions based on the information in the text. Explain that when we make inferences, we go beyond literal meaning of the story and make interpretations. Tell students that they will need to infer information in order to decide whether the statements in the exercise are true or false.

2. Have students complete the exercise. Go over the answers with the class. If there is disagreement, ask students to cite examples in the story to support their opinion.

✪✪✪ EXPRESS OPINIONS   Suggested Time: 15 minutes

Give students a few minutes to write down answers to the questions. Then initiate a whole class discussion. Make it clear that there is no right or wrong answer to the questions. However, challenge students to support their opinions with examples from the story.

Expansion/Homework

The questions in this exercise are very complex and can elicit very passionate and deep discussion. It may be more productive to work on only one or two questions in class and assign the remaining questions as homework. Students can either write a brief answer or simply prepare some points to discuss.

CRITICAL THINKING

Give students the following questions for discussion in small groups before discussing as a whole class:

1. How did Gregor's family feel about him? What evidence in the story supports your answer?

   Answer: They cared about him, but they were afraid of him. His mother fainted, but she begged the father not to kill him. His father beat Gregor back into the bedroom. His sister fed him, but she was frightened when he followed her into the dining room. They left the door to his room open for two hours each night.

2. How did Grete's feelings about Gregor change? Find evidence in the story to support your answer.

   Answer: She stopped thinking of him as a person. In the beginning, she provided food and cleaned his room, but by the end, she said they must find a way to get rid of him.

3. After time passes, does Gregor still have any human qualities or feelings? Give evidence from the story to support your answer.

   Answer: A few. He wanted the picture on his wall, he was soothed by the music, and he thought of his family tenderly.

4. How might the story be different if Gregor had turned into a butterfly instead of a cockroach?

   Answers will vary, but students should support their ideas with reasons and examples.

✦✦✦ B READING TWO: Ungeziefer

📂 Go to www.mynorthstarlab.com to read and listen to *Ungeziefer*.

Suggested Time: 20 minutes

Reading Two is a review of "The Metamorphosis" by a literary critic. It stimulates critical thinking as students read a critic's opinions of Franz Kafka and the story.

1. Read the instructions for **Exercise 1** with the class. Introduce the term *critic* and make sure students are clear about the meaning. Explain that a critic evaluates and interprets works of art, literature, and music. You may want to bring some examples of book reviews to class.

2. Explain the concept of *ungeziefer* and then have students read the article. You can also choose to play the recording of the reading and have students listen as they read.

3. Have students complete **Exercise 2** and then compare answers with a partner's. Call on individual students to share their answers with the class.

Expansion/Homework

Ask students to explain how insects are regarded in their society. Do they have a word like *ungeziefer* to describe them? Can they think of other animals with a similar symbolism as the cockroach in Kafka's story?

✿✿✿ C INTEGRATE READINGS ONE AND TWO

◖ SKILLS

Organize information from the readings in a chart; synthesize information from the readings to write an interview.

STEP 1: Organize   Suggested Time: 15 minutes

1. Tell students that they will use the information from the story in Reading One to support the critic's statements from Reading Two.

2. Have students complete the exercise. Then have them compare their answers with a partner's. Call on individual students to share their answers with the class.

STEP 2: Synthesize   Suggested Time: 20 minutes

1. Have students complete the interview individually. Encourage students to use vocabulary from the unit. Then divide the class into pairs and have students take turns role-playing their interviews.

2. If time allows, invite pairs to read their completed interviews to the class.

Expansion/Homework

Ask each student to think of at least one additional question to add to the interview. Divide the class into pairs and have students role-play the rest of the interview using each other's questions.

Link to *NorthStar: Listening and Speaking 3*

If students are also using the companion text, you might want to ask them to write a short paragraph critiquing the story "Lavender."

📁 Go to www.mynorthstarlab.com for *Notetaking* and *Academic Skills Practice*.

3 FOCUS ON WRITING

A VOCABULARY

◖ SKILLS

Review vocabulary from Readings One and Two in the context of a crossword puzzle; expand vocabulary by identifying synonyms; use new vocabulary creatively to write a descriptive paragraph.

✪ REVIEW   Suggested Time: 15 minutes

Make sure students understand how to complete the puzzle. Then have them solve it individually or with a partner. If possible, use an overhead transparency projector to review the completed puzzle.

Expansion/Homework
You can divide the class into two teams and award a small prize to the team that completes the puzzle first.

 Link to NorthStar: Listening and Speaking 3
If students are also using the companion text, you might want to have them choose vocabulary from Unit 6 of the *Listening and Speaking* strand and create crossword puzzles for their classmates to solve.

✪✪ EXPAND   Suggested Time: 15 minutes

📁 Go to www.mynorthstarlab.com for *Expand*.

1. Have students read the sentence pairs in **Exercise 1** and compare the boldfaced words. Identify the boldfaced words as synonyms and read the explanation to students.

2. Go over the instructions for **Exercise 2**. Do the first item as an example before having students complete the exercise. Review the answers as a class and discuss the variations in meaning. Offer explanations as needed.

Expansion/Homework
It can be useful to introduce students to working with a thesaurus. Ask them to pick one or two words from the exercise and look for as many additional synonyms as possible and decide how the meaning changes.

 Link to NorthStar: Listening and Speaking 3
If students are also using the companion text, you might want to select some vocabulary words from Unit 6 of the *Listening and Speaking* strand and have students find synonyms with more general or specific meanings.

VOCABULARY EXPANSION: Vocabulary Frames

Have students create flashcard vocabulary frames as shown. Tell them to write the vocabulary word on one side of the card and put the following information on the opposite side. Students can work with their partner to practice with the flashcards.

synonym		antonym
	definition	
sentence		drawing

✪ CREATE   Suggested Time: 20 minutes

Go over the instructions with the class. Then have students write a paragraph about an insect using at least five of the target vocabulary words. Call on individual students to read their paragraphs to the class.

Expansion/Homework
This activity can be done as homework and reviewed in class. Students can also choose a photograph or picture of an insect to describe.

📁 Go to www.mynorthstarlab.com for additional *Vocabulary* practice.

✦✦ B GRAMMAR: Infinitives of Purpose

📁 Go to www.mynorthstarlab.com for *Grammar Chart* and *Exercise 2*.

◖ SKILLS

Use infinitives of purpose to describe events in a story.

Suggested Time: 20 minutes

1. Have students read the sentences in **Exercise 1** and underline the verbs with the form *to* + verb. Have them identify what questions these sentences answer.

2. Introduce infinitives of purpose and go over the grammar chart.

3. Have students complete **Exercise 2** individually. Go over the answers as a class.

4. Have students complete **Exercise 3** individually. Call on individual students to read their completed sentences to the class.

Expansion/Homework
For further practice, offer exercises from *Focus on Grammar 3,* 3rd Edition or Azar's *Fundamentals of English Grammar,* 3rd Edition. See the Grammar Book References on page 219 of the student book for specific units and chapters.

📁 Go to www.mynorthstarlab.com for additional *Grammar* practice.

If you wish to assign a different writing task than the one in this section, see page 119. The Alternative Writing Topics can also be assigned as additional writing topics for homework. The alternative topics relate to the theme of the unit, but may not target the same grammar or rhetorical structures taught in the unit.

◀ SKILLS

Answer *wh-* questions; add details to a story; integrate the concepts, vocabulary, grammar, and rhetorical structures from the unit to write a story with a moral.

✪✪✪ PREPARE TO WRITE: Answering *Wh-* Questions

Suggested Time: 10 minutes

1. Explain to students that as a culminating activity, they will write a story about an insect or an animal. Go over the information in the task box with the class. Explain to students that many stories, especially fables, have morals, or practical lessons that can be learned from them. Their story should contain a moral as well.

2. Give students a few minutes to think about their story and write down answers to the *wh-* questions in **Exercise 1**. Move around the room and offer assistance if necessary. Then have students share their answers with a partner.

Expansion/Homework
The subject of animals and insects is not always popular. Allow students to choose stories on other topics as long as the story has a moral.

✪✪✪ WRITE: A Story with a Moral

Suggested Time: 30 minutes

1. Read the introduction with the class. Then have students read the story in **Exercise 1**.

2. Divide the class into groups and have students discuss the story, checking the answer that is most appropriate. Discuss the answers as a class.

3. Have students read the story in **Exercise 2** individually and complete the text with their own ending. Invite students to share their endings with the class.

4. Discuss the questions in **Exercise 3** as a class.

5. Go over the instructions for **Exercise 4** with the class. Have students complete the outline of their stories. Move around the room and offer assistance if necessary.

6. Go over the instructions for **Exercise 5** with the class. Point out traditional story openers such as *Once upon a time* or *One day* and encourage students to use them in their stories. Then have students write the first draft. You can also assign writing the first draft as homework.

✪✪✪ REVISE: Adding Detail

Suggested Time: 20 minutes

1. Invite a student to read the introductory paragraph aloud. Then go over the examples with the class. Remind students of the importance of word order when using adjectives and adverbs.

2. Have students complete the story in **Exercise 1** using the words in the box. Have students share their completed paragraphs with a classmate.

3. Go over the instructions for **Exercise 2**. Have students return to their first drafts and look for any words or phrases that could be made more interesting. Move around the room and offer suggestions.

✪✪✪ EDIT: Writing the Final Draft

Suggested Time: 20 minutes

Have students write the final draft of their paragraphs. Encourage them to use language and grammar from the unit. Make sure they go through the checklist before submitting their final drafts. Collect the paragraphs and correct them before the next class.

 Go to www.mynorthstarlab.com for *Writing the Final Draft.*

✪ ALTERNATIVE WRITING TOPICS

These topics give students an alternative opportunity to explore and write about issues related to the unit theme.

✪ RESEARCH TOPICS

Suggested Time: 20 minutes in class

1. Have students turn to page 214. Review the instructions for the activity with the class.

2. For Topic 1, you can aid story selection by arranging for students to visit a library or bookstore. You can increase student interest by giving your own presentation, including an illustration. For Topic 2, direct students to encyclopedias, science books, or the Internet. Remind students of the importance of paraphrasing information in order to avoid plagiarism.

3. Have students prepare their presentation or research findings and share them with the class or in groups. Encourage other students to ask questions.

 Go to www.mynorthstarlab.com for *Student Writing Models, Integrated Task, Video Activity, Internet Activity,* and *Unit 6 Achievement Test.*

UNIT 7

The Choice to Be Amish

Go to www.mynorthstarlab.com for the MyNorthStarLab *Readiness Check*.

① FOCUS ON THE TOPIC

◖SKILLS

Interpret a photograph; share opinions about the role of technology in modern life; interpret a timeline; infer meaning of new vocabulary from context.

✾✾✾Ⓐ PREDICT

Suggested Time: 10 minutes

1. Have students study the photograph and answer question 1. Call on students to share their answers with the class. See if anybody can identify the people as Amish. Explain briefly who the Amish are and where they live.

2. Have students answer question 2. Call on students to share their choices with the class. Encourage discussion.

✾✾Ⓑ SHARE INFORMATION

Suggested Time: 15 minutes

Divide the class into small groups and have students rank the items in order of importance. Then ask each group to share their rankings with the class and create a whole class survey on the board. Encourage students to explain the reasons for their ranking.

✾✾✾Ⓒ BACKGROUND AND VOCABULARY

 Go to www.mynorthstarlab.com for *Background and Vocabulary*.

Suggested Time: 20 minutes

1. Read the introductory paragraph with the class. Then have students look at the map and call out places where the Amish live. Then ask students if they can think of any other religious groups that lead a life outside mainstream society.

2. Have students read the timeline in **Exercise 1** without worrying about new vocabulary items. Then have them read the text again attempting to understand the boldfaced words.

3. Have students complete **Exercise 2** in pairs or individually. Then review the answers with the class. Explain any other unfamiliar vocabulary.

Go to www.mynorthstarlab.com for additional *Background and Vocabulary* practice.

②FOCUS ON READING

◖ SKILLS

Read for main ideas and details; infer opinions based on the information in the text; express personal opinions; support opinions with reasons.

❖❖❖ Ⓐ READING ONE: The Amish

 Go to www.mynorthstarlab.com to read and listen to *The Amish*.

Suggested Time: 20 minutes

Reading One is an article that appeared in *American Religion* magazine. It describes the Amish way of life and customs, and consequences some of the Amish face when they decide to leave the community.

Ask students to read the article individually, paying special attention to the boldfaced words they learned in the previous exercise. Move around the room and explain any unfamiliar vocabulary as needed. The reading can be assigned as homework or lab work using MyNorthStarLab. You can also choose to play the recording of the reading and have students listen as they read.

READING STRATEGY: Organizing Information

1. Explain to students that there are many ways to organize the information they read, including various graphic organizers, folds, and charts. For this activity, have students divide a page into four equal columns.

2. In the first column, have students draw pictures, symbols, or illustrations of Amish life. In the next three columns, have students organize the information in paragraphs 2, 3, and 4 under three headings which might include topics like culture, work, families, beliefs, customs, or issues.

3. After the information is organized, have students compare their choices in small groups and add or revise information. Then have students share choices as a class.

❖❖❖ READ FOR MAIN IDEAS   **Suggested Time: 15 minutes**

Have students complete the exercise individually. Go over the answers as a class. If there are disagreements, ask students to scan the text for passages that support their answers.

✪✪✪ READ FOR DETAILS

1. If necessary, have students read the article again. Go over the instructions for the exercise with the class. Make sure students understand that they have to cross out the details that are not included in the reading.

2. Have students complete the exercise. Go over the answers as a class. If students disagree on a detail, challenge them to find details in the text to support their claims.

REACHING ALL STUDENTS: Read for Details	
• **Less Proficient:** Help students to locate details by having them locate key words from the details and connecting those with a specific paragraph.	• **More Proficient:** Suggest that students research the Amish to list three more details about their lifestyle, which they can discuss in one or two paragraphs.

✪✪✪ MAKE INFERENCES

Suggested Time: 15 minutes

1. Go over the instructions with students. Explain that they will need to decide which statements would possibly be made by a person who has left the Amish community and which by a person who has stayed based on the information in the article. Then have students complete the exercise.

2. Have students discuss their answers with a partner. Move around the room and listen to the conversations.

Expansion/Homework
This exercise is good practice for the TOEFL iBT. You may want to time the questions in order to simulate test conditions. Refer to *NorthStar Building Skills for the TOEFL iBT Intermediate* for more practice for the TOEFL iBT.

✪✪✪ EXPRESS OPINIONS

Suggested Time: 15 minutes

With the same partners as in the previous exercise, have students discuss their own opinions about the quotations in Make Inferences. Move around the room and listen to the conversations. Ask questions to help students focus their answers.

Expansion/Homework
The quotations in this exercise are very controversial to many students and may make them feel uncomfortable to discuss. For other students, the statements may trigger a very heated debate. Rather than discussing all the quotations with partners, you may prefer dividing the class into groups and allow them to select one or two of the quotations to discuss.

Link to *NorthStar: Listening and Speaking 3*

If students are also using the companion text, you can have them discuss the similarities and differences between the Amish and the urban homesteaders.

CRITICAL THINKING

Give students the following questions for discussion in small groups before discussing as a whole class:

1. What words or phrases best describe the Amish?

   Answers will vary, but might include: simple, religious, pious, hard working, reclusive.

2. Do you think their decision to keep to the old European ways is good? Why or why not?

   Answers will vary, but students should support their responses with convincing explanations.

3. Do you agree with their practice of shunning those who leave the community? Explain.

   Answers will vary, but students should support their opinions with convincing explanations.

4. What criticisms would the Amish have of our modern lifestyles? Support your answers with information from the text.

   Answers will vary, but students should support their responses with information from the text.

✿✿✿ B READING TWO: A Decision to Leave

 Go to www.mynorthstarlab.com to read and listen to *A Decision to Leave*.

Suggested Time: 20 minutes

Reading Two is an article about Isaac Schlabach, an Amish man who decided to leave the Amish community to live in the outside world.

1. Tell students that in **Exercise 1**, they will read a true story about a man who left the Amish community before *rumspringa*.

2. Have students read the article. You can also choose to play the recording of the reading and have students listen as they read. Then have students answer the questions in **Exercise 2**. Call on individual students to share their answers. If there are any disagreements, ask students to find information from the text that supports their answers.

INTEGRATE READINGS ONE AND TWO

◖ SKILLS

Support main ideas from Reading One with details from Reading Two; synthesize information from the readings to complete a letter.

STEP 1: Organize   Suggested Time: 15 minutes

1. Go over the instructions with the class. Make sure students understand the task.

2. Have students read the outline and then find details from Reading Two to support each main idea from Reading One. Call on students to share their answers with the class.

STEP 2: Synthesize   Suggested Time: 15 minutes

1. Go over the instructions with the class. Tell students to use information from Step 1 to complete the letter.

2. Have students complete the letter individually. Invite a few students to read their letters to the class. Encourage the class to offer additional ideas or corrections.

Expansion/Homework
For homework, ask students to write a letter from an Amish leader to a young person who is thinking of leaving the community.

 Go to www.mynorthstarlab.com for *Notetaking* and *Academic Skills Practice*.

③ FOCUS ON WRITING

A VOCABULARY

◖ SKILLS

Review vocabulary from Readings One and Two by identifying synonyms and antonyms; expand vocabulary by learning new idioms; use new vocabulary creatively to write a summary.

⊙ REVIEW

Suggested Time: 10 minutes

 Go to www.mynorthstarlab.com for *Review.*

1. Explain to students that two words in each item are synonyms with the boldfaced word and one word in each item is an antonym. Have students decide which word doesn't belong in each group and cross it out.

2. Go over the answers with the class and explain the meaning of any vocabulary that is still unclear.

Expansion/Homework

Encourage students to use a thesaurus and read about other words with a meaning close to or related to the boldfaced word.

⊙⊙ EXPAND

Suggested Time: 15 minutes

1. Have students read the passage in **Exercise 1** paying special attention to the boldfaced phrases.

2. Have students complete **Exercise 2**. Go over the answers as a class.

Expansion/Homework

If time remains, have students break up into pairs and take turns making sentences with the new idioms. Encourage students to keep a vocabulary journal with lists of idioms and their definitions.

VOCABULARY EXPANSION: Context Clues

1. Tell students that the meaning of words is often found directly in the text in the form of synonyms, antonyms, definitions, or general clues.

2. Give students the following words and have them locate the meaning in the text: *immigrants, the Amish, Pennsylvania Dutch, shunning, rumspringa,* and *settle down.* Have students indicate whether the meaning is given as a synonym, a definition, or by clues. To extend the activity, ask students to write their own sentences with the words.

⊙ CREATE

Suggested Time: 25 minutes

1. Explain to students that everyone has to make difficult decisions in the course of their life. Provide an example from your own life if you wish to. Then read the example paragraph with the class.

2. Brainstorm possible questions students can ask their partners. Write the questions on the board. Then divide the class into pairs and have students take turns asking each other about difficult decisions in their lives.

3. Have students write a one-paragraph summary of what they learned. Encourage them to use vocabulary from the unit, especially the new idioms. Alternatively, you can assign the writing part of the exercise as homework and have students share their paragraph in the next class.

Link to *NorthStar: Listening and Speaking 3*
If students are also using the companion text, you might want to have students imagine they have made a decision to become urban homesteaders and write a paragraph about the experience.

Go to www.mynorthstarlab.com for additional *Vocabulary* practice.

B GRAMMAR: Noun Clauses with *Wh-* Words

Go to www.mynorthstarlab.com for *Grammar Chart* and *Exercise 3*.

◖ SKILLS

Learn about and use noun clauses with *wh-* words.

Suggested Time: 30 minutes

1. Have students read the paragraph in **Exercise 1** and elicit what they already know about the structure of the boldfaced clauses (they begin with *wh-* words).

2. Call on individual students to come to the board, copy the sentences from **Exercise 2**, and label the boldfaced parts. Encourage other students to correct any errors.

3. Review the grammar chart with the class and ask individual students to read the examples.

4. Divide the class into pairs. Have students read the conversation and complete the sentences in **Exercise 3**. Call on students to read their complete sentences to the class. Encourage other students to correct any errors.

5. With the same partner, have students complete the questions in **Exercise 4**, using information from the readings. Call on individual students to share their sentences with the class.

Expansion/Homework
(1) You may want to assign Exercise 4 as homework and go over the questions in the next class. (2) For further practice, offer exercises from *Focus on Grammar 3*, 3rd Edition or Azar's *Fundamentals of English Grammar*, 3rd Edition. See the Grammar Book References on page 219 of the student book for specific units and chapters.

Go to www.mynorthstarlab.com for additional *Grammar* practice.

If you wish to assign a different writing task than the one in this section, see page 142. The Alternative Writing Topics can also be assigned as additional writing topics for homework. The alternative topics relate to the theme of the unit, but may not target the same grammar or rhetorical structures taught in the unit.

◀ SKILLS

Ask question as a pre-writing technique; create an outline; use parallel structure in an essay; integrate the concepts, vocabulary, grammar, and rhetorical structures from the unit to write an essay about a difficult decision.

✪✪✪ PREPARE TO WRITE: Asking Yourself Questions

Suggested Time: 10 minutes

1. Explain to students that as a culminating activity, they will write an essay about a difficult decision they had to make in their life. If students are extremely reluctant to share personal information, allow them to choose a different example of a difficult decision to write about.

2. Have students answer the questions about the decision. Move around the room, helping students and asking for clarification where appropriate.

✪✪✪ WRITE: An Outline

Suggested Time: 35 minutes

1. Elicit from students the structure of a paragraph. Explain that this structure can be extended to apply to an entire essay. Go over the example outline with the class.

2. Have students read the essay in **Exercise 1** and discuss the questions that follow the essay with a classmate. Invite individual students to share their answers with the class.

3. Next, have students complete the outline in **Exercise 2** with information from the essay. Then have them compare their outlines with a partner's.

4. Go over the instructions in **Exercise 3** and have students complete an outline for their own essay. Move around the room and offer assistance as necessary. Then have students write the first draft. You can also assign writing the first draft as homework.

✪✪✪ REVISE: Using Parallel Structure

Suggested Time: 25 minutes

1. Have students read the sentences in **Exercise 1** and label the subjects and verbs. Call on individual students to read the words they underlined. Correct any mistakes.

2. Introduce the concept of parallel structure and read through the explanations and examples in the chart. Explain to students that one way to check for errors in parallel structure is to identify items in a sentence, write them vertically on a page, and then compare their forms.

3. Have students complete **Exercise 2** individually. Go over the answers as a class. Encourage students to correct each other if they recognize mistakes.

4. Have students complete the paragraph in **Exercise 3** with the appropriate word forms. Invite students to read their paragraphs to the class.

5. Go over the instructions for **Exercise 4** and have students return to the first draft of their essays and rewrite sentences to include parallel structure where appropriate. Move around the room and give tips on where parallel structures might be appropriate.

✪✪✪ EDIT: Writing the Final Draft

Suggested Time: 20 minutes

Have students write the final draft of their essays. Encourage them to use language and grammar from the unit. Make sure they go through the checklist before submitting their final drafts. Collect the essays and correct them before the next class.

 Go to www.mynorthstarlab.com for *Writing the Final Draft*.

✪ ALTERNATIVE WRITING TOPICS

These topics give students an alternative opportunity to explore and write about issues related to the unit theme.

✪ RESEARCH TOPICS

Suggested Time: 20 minutes in class

1. Have students turn to page 214. Review the instructions for the activity with the class.

2. Have students choose one community or person from the list and research it in the library or on the Internet. Emphasize that students' research should include answers to the questions listed in the book. Encourage students to include additional information they find.

3. Have students write a report about the community or person they researched and present it to the class or in small groups.

 Go to www.mynorthstarlab.com for *Student Writing Models, Integrated Task, Video Activity, Internet Activity*, and *Unit 7 Achievement Test*.

UNIT 8

Finding a Spouse

OVERVIEW

Theme: Marriage

This unit introduces the topic of marriage and explains how choosing a spouse and courtship vary in different cultures. Students explore the topic, express their personal opinions about marriage customs, and write a descriptive essay using information from the unit.

Reading One: *Finding a Spouse* is an article from a journal of anthropology about courtship and selection of a mate in various cultures.

Reading Two: *What's Wrong with Tradition?* is a letter from a Vietnamese student in America to a university newspaper defending his country's traditional way of choosing spouses.

Critical Thinking

Identify personal assumptions about marriage

Differentiate between main ideas and details

Evaluate information in the text according to personal beliefs

Match traditions to cultures

Rank cultural practices on a continuum

Classify information

Reading

Make predictions

Identify main ideas

Read for details

Make inferences based on information from a text

Organize and synthesize information from the readings

Writing

Complete a summary

Describe a cultural tradition of courtship

Categorize ideas for writing

Use related word forms for cohesion

Write a point-by-point paragraph

Write an essay describing important characteristics in a spouse or partner

Vocabulary

Use context clues to find meaning

Define words

Identify analogies and word forms

Grammar

Definite and indefinite articles

 MyNorthStarLab
Readiness Check, Background and Vocabulary, Readings One and Two, Notetaking and Academic Skills Practice, Vocabulary and Grammar, Writing the Final Draft, Achievement Test

 NorthStar: Listening and Speaking 3
Unit 8 explores responsibilities and expectations in a marriage, with special consideration to prenuptial agreements.

Go to www.mynorthstarlab.com for the MyNorthStarLab *Readiness Check*.

① FOCUS ON THE TOPIC

◖ SKILLS

Interpret a joke; share opinions and personal values about marriage; infer meaning of new vocabulary from context.

✿✿✿ Ⓐ PREDICT

Suggested Time: 10 minutes

Read the joke with the class. Call on students to offer their interpretations of the joke. Then discuss the questions with the class.

✿✿ Ⓑ SHARE INFORMATION

Suggested Time: 15 minutes

Have students rank the reasons for marriage and discuss their choices with a partner. Then call on individual students to share their ranking with the class. Encourage students to add other reasons not mentioned in the book.

✿✿✿ Ⓒ BACKGROUND AND VOCABULARY

Go to www.mynorthstarlab.com for *Background and Vocabulary*.

Suggested Time: 20 minutes

1. Explain to students that they will take a short quiz on their knowledge of marriage customs around the world. Have students complete **Exercise 1** matching cultures to customs. Explain that there can be more than one correct choice. Give students the answers from the Answer Key. Ask them to explain which items surprised them the most.

2. Have students complete **Exercise 2** in pairs or individually. Then review the answers with the class. Explain any other unfamiliar vocabulary.

Expansion/Homework
If students are from one of the cultures mentioned in Exercise 1, ask them if they know or practice these customs. For students from other cultures, invite them to share their own customs.

Go to www.mynorthstarlab.com for additional *Background and Vocabulary* practice.

②FOCUS ON READING

◀ SKILLS

Predict the content by relating it to personal experience; read for main ideas; answer questions about details; infer information from the reading to complete a number scale; express personal opinions about marriage customs; read a letter.

✪✪✪ Ⓐ READING ONE: Finding a Spouse

📂 Go to www.mynorthstarlab.com to read and listen to *Finding a Spouse*.

Suggested Time: 25 minutes

Reading One is an article from a magazine for anthropology students. It introduces the readers to marriage customs of the Chinese and Hopi, as well as the Oneida community of New York and the Mormons. The reading gives students an opportunity to familiarize themselves with a style of an academic journal.

1. Go over the definition of *anthropology* as you read the introduction. Next, have students read the questions. Then have them share their answers with a partner. Call on individual students to share their answers with the rest of the class.

2. Have students read the article. The reading can be assigned as homework or lab work using MyNorthStarLab. You can also choose to play the recording of the reading and have students listen as they read.

READING STRATEGY: Summarizing

1. Tell students that creating a pyramid organizer can help them with summaries. At the point of the pyramid, summarize the paragraph in one word. Just below it, add another word, and below that, three words, then four, then five, then six until a full summary of the piece is contained in the pyramid.

2. Model paragraph 2 in pyramid form as follows: *marriage, Chinese families, used a matchmaker, older family members decided, goal was to produce sons, to keep the family name alive, to become leaders in the family.* Then have student groups of four create pyramid summaries on large chart paper to share with the class for paragraphs 3, 4, 5, and 6. They can then use their pyramid to write a summary paragraph in their own words.

✪✪✪ READ FOR MAIN IDEAS   Suggested Time: 10 minutes

Have students complete the matching exercise and then compare their answers with a partner's. As you discuss the answers with the class, point out that many of the cultural beliefs are traditional and may no longer be true.

Expansion/Homework

If students know other marriage customs from their home country or anywhere else in the world, invite them to share those customs with the class. Write the customs on the board.

✪✪✪ READ FOR DETAILS   Suggested Time: 15 minutes

1. If necessary, have students read the article again. Then tell students that not all answers to the questions need to be complete sentences.

2. Have students write the answers individually. Then have them compare answers with a partner's. While checking answers, have pairs discuss any answers that differ until they can agree on the correct answer. Then ask students to share their answers with the class. Offer clarification as needed.

✪✪✪ MAKE INFERENCES   Suggested Time: 15 minutes

1. Read the instructions with the class. Explain to students that the number line represents a scale and that they have to decide what number each culture should be assigned based on what they read in the article. Tell students that this is an inferencing task—the answers are not explicitly stated in the text, but they will need to be concluded based on the information in the reading.

2. Have students complete the task and then discuss their choices in small groups. Call on individual students to share their answers with the class. Encourage discussion.

Expansion/Homework

Have students research other cultures and their marriage customs, and assign a number from the scale. In class, have students present their findings.

✪✪✪ EXPRESS OPINIONS   Suggested Time: 15 minutes

Divide the class into pairs and have students discuss the pros and cons of the customs in the list. Move around the room and ask questions to encourage discussion.

REACHING ALL STUDENTS: Express Opinions	
• **Less Proficient:** Help students to prepare for discussion by first having partners work together to connect the practice to the cultural group (for example, Chinese—choices were made by elders).	• **More Proficient:** Suggest that students write a paragraph expressing their views on each topic after the discussions.

Give students the following questions for discussion in small groups before discussing as a whole class:

1. Which cultural or religious groups are discussed in the article?

   Answer: Chinese, Hopi, Old Bavarian, Oneida, and Early Mormon

2. Why do you think the Hopi and the Bavarians allowed relationships between such young partners?

   Answers will vary, but students might suggest that they needed to produce many children, life expectancy was shorter, infant mortality was greater.

3. Which method do you think is the best for creating a successful marriage?

   Answers will vary, but students should support their opinions from their knowledge and the text.

4. Which method do you think is the least likely to create a successful marriage?

   Answers will vary, but students should support their opinions from their knowledge and the information in the text.

 Link to *NorthStar: Listening and Speaking 3*

If students are also using the companion text, you might ask them to discuss which of the cultures in Reading One might favor writing a prenuptial agreement and what they would include in it. Have students use information from the reading to support their ideas.

B READING TWO: What's Wrong with Tradition?

Go to www.mynorthstarlab.com to read and listen to *What's Wrong with Tradition?*

Suggested Time: 20 minutes

Reading Two extends the topic of marriage as students read a letter to the editor, in which a Vietnamese student defends arranged marriages.

1. Remind students that a letter to the editor is a letter written by a newspaper reader that expresses his or her ideas or opinions about a topic. Tell students that they will read a letter to the editor written by a Vietnamese student expressing his opinions about marriage customs in his country.

2. Have students read the letter in **Exercise 1**. You can also choose to play the recording of the reading and have students listen as they read. Then have them complete **Exercise 2**. Call on individual students to read their answers to the class.

◖SKILLS

Organize information from the readings in a chart; synthesize information from the readings to complete a summary.

STEP 1: Organize   Suggested Time: 15 minutes

Go over the instructions and the example with the class. Then have students complete the chart. Call on individual students to share their answers with the class. If there is any disagreement, ask students to point to the appropriate statements in the readings that support their answers.

Expansion/Homework
If you have an overhead projector or computer projector available, display the chart on the board and invite students to come to the front and fill in the lines for each custom.

STEP 2: Synthesize   Suggested Time: 15 minutes

Have students complete the study guide with information from the chart in Step 1. Invite students to read their answers to the class. If students don't agree, encourage them to speak up and challenge their classmates.

 Go to www.mynorthstarlab.com for *Notetaking* and *Academic Skills Practice*.

③FOCUS ON WRITING

Ⓐ VOCABULARY

◖SKILLS

Review vocabulary from Readings One and Two; expand vocabulary by organizing vocabulary by category and showing relationships reflecting these categories; use new vocabulary creatively to write a descriptive paragraph.

✪ REVIEW   Suggested Time: 15 minutes

 Go to www.mynorthstarlab.com for *Review*.

1. Ask a student to read the short paragraph on courtship and review the terms *courtship, wedding ceremony,* and *married life.*

2. Individually, have students read the sentences and decide which phase of a relationship they belong to. Review the answers as a class. Encourage discussion and ask students to give examples to support their answers.

✪✪ EXPAND

Suggested Time: 15 minutes

1. Review the categories and definitions with the class and go over the examples.

2. Have students complete the exercise individually and review their answers with a classmate. Then call on individual students to read their answers to the class.

VOCABULARY EXPANSION: Act Out a Word

1. Having students role-play or act out a word is a good strategy to promote retention of vocabulary with a fun activity. One group acts out the word and the other groups attempt to guess the word and its meaning.

2. Have students work in groups of four (of mixed proficiency) to draw one of these vocabulary words from a bowl or bag: *spouse, romantic, pregnant, polygamy, leadership, proud, faithful*. After students act out the word, groups should take a minute to discuss before attempting a guess of the word rather than calling out random guesses.

Link to *NorthStar: Listening and Speaking 3*
If students are also using the companion text, you might have them choose five words from Unit 8 of the *Listening and Speaking* strand and use them to create these analogies: synonyms, antonyms, cause/effect, degree, and related.

✪ CREATE

Suggested Time: 25 minutes

Have students brainstorm courtship rituals from their culture and write a descriptive paragraph using at least five words from the box. If the students do not have information about courtship traditions, allow them to write about courtship in general.

 Go to www.mynorthstarlab.com for additional *Vocabulary* practice.

✪✪ B GRAMMAR: Definite and Indefinite Articles

 Go to www.mynorthstarlab.com for *Grammar Chart* and *Exercise 2*.

◖ SKILLS

Identify and correctly use definite and indefinite articles.

Suggested Time: 25 minutes

1. Have students read the paragraph in **Exercise 1** and underline the definite articles and circle the indefinite articles.

2. Review the grammar chart with the class and ask individual students to read the examples. This is a difficult topic for many students as many languages do not distinguish between definite and indefinite articles, and some languages have no articles at all. Offer plenty of examples to make sure students understand the concept.

3. Have students complete the paragraph in **Exercise 2** and compare their answers with a partner's. Then call on individual students to read parts of the paragraph to the class. Correct any mistakes.

4. Have students complete **Exercise 3** individually and review the answers with the class.

5. Go over the instructions for **Exercise 4**. Ask students to think of a wedding they have attended and write a short paragraph describing it. Remind students to pay special attention to the correct use of articles.

Expansion/Homework

(**1**) You might want to assign Exercise 4 as homework and review answers in class. (**2**) For further practice, offer exercises from *Focus on Grammar 3,* 3rd Edition or Azar's *Fundamentals of English Grammar,* 3rd Edition. See the Grammar Book References on page 219 of the student book for specific units and chapters.

 Go to www.mynorthstarlab.com for additional *Grammar* practice.

ⓒ WRITING

If you wish to assign a different writing task than the one in this section, see page 161. The Alternative Writing Topics can also be assigned as additional writing topics for homework. The alternative topics relate to the theme of the unit, but may not target the same grammar or rhetorical structures taught in the unit.

◖ SKILLS

Categorize information; use cohesive devices in writing; integrate the concepts, vocabulary, grammar, and rhetorical structures from the unit to write an essay with point-by-point structure.

✪✪✪ PREPARE TO WRITE: Categorizing

Suggested Time: 10 minutes

1. Explain to students that as a culminating activity, they will write a descriptive essay. Go over the information in the task box with the class.

2. Go over the instructions for **Exercise 1** with the class. Divide the class into small groups and have students brainstorm characteristics that are important in a spouse or partner.

3. Have students work individually to complete **Exercise 2**. Have students choose the characteristics they feel are most important and group them into categories such as appearance, personality, etc.

4. Go over the instructions for **Exercise 3** with the class. Have students choose the two most important categories, and within each category, the three most important characteristics. Call on individual students to share their choices with the class.

Expansion/Homework
As an alternative to simple lists, allow students to use mind maps or other graphic organizers to express their categorization.

✪✪✪ WRITE: A Point-by-Point Paragraph

Suggested Time: 30 minutes

1. Ask a student to read the short explanation of point-by-point structure. Explain that point-by-point structure applies to both paragraphs and full essays.

2. Have students read the paragraph in **Exercise 1** and discuss the questions with a partner.

3. Go over the instructions for **Exercise 2** and have student complete the task. Call on individual students to read the transition words which show degree of importance.

4. Have students read the instructions for **Exercise 3** and complete the task. Have them return to the categories and characteristics they defined in Prepare to Write, rank each characteristic in order of importance, and write a short explanation of their reasons for choosing these characteristics. Move around the room and offer assistance where necessary.

5. Go over the instructions for **Exercise 4** with the class. Then have students write a first draft of their essay. You can also assign writing the first draft as homework.

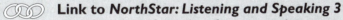 **Link to *NorthStar: Listening and Speaking 3***
If students are also using the companion text, encourage them to use vocabulary and ideas from Unit 8 of the *Listening and Speaking* strand in their essays.

✪✪✪ REVISE: Using Related Word Forms for Cohesion

Suggested Time: 25 minutes

1. Introduce the concept of cohesion to students. Then have them read the sample paragraphs in **Exercise 1** and look for what makes them cohesive. After a few minutes, elicit ideas from students. Then call on a student to read the explanation in the box. Remind students of the word form exercises they have done in previous units.

2. Have students complete the paragraph in **Exercise 2** using the appropriate forms of the words in the box. Then call on individual students to read one sentence each. The rest of the class listens and offers corrections where appropriate. If you have an overhead projector or computer projector, invite students to the front of the class to write their answers directly onto the board.

3. Have students read the instructions for **Exercise 3** and then go back to their first drafts and add related words to make their essays more cohesive. Move around the room and offer assistance where necessary.

✪✪✪ EDIT: Writing the Final Draft

Suggested Time: 20 minutes

Have students write the final draft of their essays. Encourage them to use language and grammar from the unit. Make sure they go through the checklist before submitting their final drafts. Collect the essays and correct them before the next class.

 Go to www.mynorthstarlab.com for *Writing the Final Draft.*

✪ ALTERNATIVE WRITING TOPICS

These topics give students an alternative opportunity to explore and write about issues related to the unit theme.

✪ RESEARCH TOPICS

Suggested Time: 25 minutes in class

1. Have students turn to page 215. Review the instructions for the activity with the class. You might want to bring in newspapers and magazines to show the class. If possible, bring in a bridal magazine. Make sure students understand the task. If possible, show an example of each item on the list.

2. Have students complete their research at home and write a summary.

3. Have students share their summaries in small groups. Move around the room, taking note of interesting findings that can be shared with the whole class.

 Link to *NorthStar: Listening and Speaking 3*
If students are also using the companion text, have them search for information related to prenuptial agreements and add it to their research.

 Go to www.mynorthstarlab.com for *Student Writing Models, Integrated Task, Video Activity, Internet Activity,* and *Unit 8 Achievement Test.*

Is Our Climate Changing?

OVERVIEW

Theme: Climate change

This unit explores the geopolitical aspects of climate change. It presents official reactions to the climate crisis and international and national government policy on climate change. Students explore the causes and effects of global warming and write an essay on how global warming affects the community.

Reading One: *Our Climate Is Changing* ... is a series of readings that report on causes and effects of climate change.

Reading Two: *Climate Change: Making Informed Decisions* is a newspaper editorial describing two sides of the debate on the issue of global warming.

Critical Thinking

Interpret illustrations

Infer word meaning from context

Differentiate between main ideas and details

Classify data

Understand and describe a scientific process

Understand and complete a causal chain

Summarize cause and effect relationships

Reading

Identify main ideas

Read for details

Infer author's position

Relate the readings to personal opinions

Organize ideas from the readings into a causal chain

Writing

Rewrite inaccurate statements

Draw a causal chain

Use cause-and-effect transitions

Use adverbial conjunctions to show cause

Use transitions to show effect

Write a cause-and-effect essay

Vocabulary

Use context clues to find meaning

Identify and use correct word forms

Identify collocations

Grammar

Future possibility: *May, might, could*

 MyNorthStarLab

Readiness Check, Background and Vocabulary, Readings One and Two, Notetaking and Academic Skills Practice, Vocabulary and Grammar, Writing the Final Draft, Achievement Test

 NorthStar: Listening and Speaking 3

Unit 9 explores how individual action to reduce one's carbon footprint can have an impact on climate change.

Go to www.mynorthstarlab.com for the MyNorthStarLab *Readiness Check*.

①FOCUS ON THE TOPIC

◖ SKILLS

Share opinions about climate change and global warming; understand a scientific process; infer meaning of new vocabulary from context.

❖❖❖Ⓐ PREDICT

Suggested Time: 10 minutes

Focus students on the photograph of the Earth and have them discuss the questions in small groups. Then call on individual students to share their group's ideas. Encourage class discussion.

❖❖Ⓑ SHARE INFORMATION

Suggested Time: 15 minutes

Have students complete the exercise individually and then share their answers with a classmate. Survey student opinions with a show of hands. Invite students to share why they agree or disagree with each statement.

❖❖❖Ⓒ BACKGROUND AND VOCABULARY

 Go to www.mynorthstarlab.com for *Background and Vocabulary*.

Suggested Time: 25 minutes

1. Explain to students that the illustrations and captions illustrate the process of climate change.

2. Tell students to read the text in **Exercise 1** without worrying about new vocabulary items. Then have students read the text again attempting to understand the boldfaced words.

3. Have students complete the definitions in **Exercise 2**. Go over the answers with the class.

Expansion/Homework
In this unit, students are exposed to a lot of very topic-specific vocabulary. As a class, you can create a mind map to organize the vocabulary and elicit additional terms from students.

② FOCUS ON READING

◖ SKILLS

Read for main ideas and details; identify inaccurate statements and rewrite them; make inferences based on details from the text; express personal opinions about climate change; read an editorial.

✱✱✱ Ⓐ READING ONE: Our Climate Is Changing ...

Go to www.mynorthstarlab.com to read and listen to *Our Climate Is Changing....*

Suggested Time: 25 minutes

Reading One is a series of articles that present the causes and effects of global warming, possible results of climate change, and statistics on CO_2 emissions.

1. Have students read the titles of the articles and the main headings and predict what they will learn after reading the articles. Write their predictions on the board.

2. Have students read the articles. Encourage them to take notes as they read. Move around the room and explain any unfamiliar vocabulary if needed. After students finish reading, ask them if their predictions were correct. The reading can be assigned as homework or lab work using MyNorthStarLab. You can also choose to play the recording of the readings and have students listen as they read.

READING STRATEGY: Summary Frames

Because students respond well to writing models, providing the following frame for students to complete will help them to understand the kind of information usually provided in summaries. Allow time for students to complete the paragraph and then discuss the components of the summary.

This New Zealand government brochure explores the problem of _____ which is caused by increased _____ in the _____. We can slow climate change, but we cannot stop it because we have already _____. The result is that the world is getting _____ and more _____. Three gases, _____, _____, and _____, are responsible for this change. They are called _____, and even if we cut their emissions by _____, the world will still _____. But if we act soon _____.

✪✪✪ READ FOR MAIN IDEAS

Suggested Time: 15 minutes

1. Go over the instructions and the example with the class. Then have students rewrite the false statements to make them true.

2. Invite students to share their new statements with the class. If students disagree, ask them to find evidence in the reading to support their statements.

✪✪✪ READ FOR DETAILS

Suggested Time: 15 minutes

1. If necessary, have students read the articles again. Then have students match the beginning and end of each sentence. Remind students that there can be more than one correct answer.

2. Call on students and have them read their combined sentences. Encourage students to present alternative combinations as well.

✪✪✪ MAKE INFERENCES

Suggested Time: 15 minutes

1. Explain that political reports are rarely completely neutral. Ask students to read the questions and identify the underlying position of the New Zealand government.

2. Call on individual students to share answers with the class. If students disagree, ask them to find evidence in the reading to support their answers. Encourage discussion.

REACHING ALL STUDENTS: Make Inferences

• **Less Proficient:** Help students with inferences by having them find two sentences from the text to directly support each inference.	• **More Proficient:** Suggest that students work with a partner to make two inferences regarding climate change in the future and support each with two sentences from the text. Students might also work in reverse, beginning with two sentences from which they can draw a conclusion or make an inference.

Expansion/Homework

(**1**) Have students research additional reports from English-speaking countries or international organizations who publish their reports in English. Do they draw similar conclusions or have a related message? (**2**) This exercise is good practice for the TOEFL iBT. You may want to time the questions in order to simulate test conditions. Refer to *NorthStar Building Skills for the TOEFL iBT Intermediate* for more practice for the TOEFL iBT.

Invite a student to read the questions aloud. Then discuss them with the class. You can initiate the discussion with an opinion of your own. Facilitate the discussion by adding comments. Make sure as many students as possible participate in the discussion. For large classes, you may want to either limit the discussion to one question or divide the class up into three groups, with each group discussing only one question.

Link to *NorthStar: Listening and Speaking 3*

If students are also using the companion text, you might want to bring the topic of personal responsibilities towards the environment to the discussion. Have students use the information from Listenings One and Two in Unit 9 of the *Listening and Speaking* strand.

CRITICAL THINKING

Give students the following questions for discussion in small groups before discussing as a whole class:

1. How is the climate changing?

Answer: It is getting hotter and more energetic.

2. What evidence shows us that humans are causing climate change?

Answer: An increase in CO_2 coupled with rising temperature

3. How do you feel about your future after reading this information?

Answers will vary, but students should give specific support for their feelings.

4. What conclusions can you draw from the chart of carbon dioxide emissions by country?

Answers will vary, but should reflect actual data from the chart to support conclusions.

B READING TWO: Climate Change: Making Informed Decisions

Go to www.mynorthstarlab.com to read and listen to *Climate Change: Making Informed Decisions*.

Suggested Time: 20 minutes

Reading Two is an editorial that describes two sides of the debate on global warming—one in support of the view that humans contribute to global warming and the other opposing it. It also stresses the importance of making informed decisions about the issue as scientific information can be easily affected by special interest.

1. Have students read the editorial in **Exercise 1**. Make sure students understand that an editorial expresses a writer's opinion on an issue. You can also choose to play the recording of the reading and have students listen as they read.

2. Review any vocabulary that may be unclear and have students complete **Exercise 2**. Call on students for answers. If there is disagreement, ask students to find excerpts from the passage that support their answers.

Expansion/Homework

Some commentators say that the Earth is doing just fine—it is the human race that is in trouble. Discuss this statement with the class.

✲✲✲ Ⓒ INTEGRATE READINGS ONE AND TWO

◖ SKILLS

Organize information from the readings in a causal chain; summarize a cause-and-effect relationship using information from the readings.

STEP 1: Organize   Suggested Time: 15 minutes

1. Introduce the concepts of cause, effect, and a causal chain. Have students refer back to Readings One and Two and find information to complete the causal chains. Move around the room and provide help where necessary.

2. While students are working, draw the incomplete causal chain on the board. Use an overhead projector, computer projector, or whiteboard if available.

3. When they are finished, invite individual students to the front of the class to fill in the missing information. Encourage the class to correct any mistakes.

STEP 2: Synthesize   Suggested Time: 20 minutes

1. Give students a few minutes to read the beginning of each summary. Then, using the information from the causal chain, have them complete each passage.

2. Have students compare their passages with a partner's. Invite individual students to read their passages to the class. Encourage classmates to make corrections or add information where appropriate.

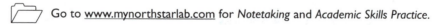 Go to www.mynorthstarlab.com for *Notetaking* and *Academic Skills Practice*.

Expansion/Homework

(**1**) The exercise can be assigned as homework, with class time used for sharing paragraphs. (**2**) Divide the class into small groups and have students create a board game based on climate change. Players move forward and backward by making *if/then* decisions based on the information in the readings and the causal chain.

FOCUS ON WRITING

 VOCABULARY

◖ SKILLS

Review vocabulary from Readings One and Two; apply vocabulary learned in the unit to a new context—an informative essay; expand vocabulary by identifying collocations; use new vocabulary creatively to write a paragraph about climate change.

✪ REVIEW   Suggested Time: 15 minutes

Go to www.mynorthstarlab.com for *Review*.

1. Have students read the story and fill in the gaps with words from the box.

2. Invite students to take turns reading sentences from the completed story. Encourage students to correct each other if there are mistakes.

Expansion/Homework

For additional practice, ask students to find synonyms, antonyms, or related terms for at least five of the words in the box.

✪✪ EXPAND   Suggested Time: 15 minutes

1. Remind students that adjectives modify nouns. Explain that not all adjective-noun combinations make sense. Tell students that they will need to match adjectives to nouns based on the context of the unit.

2. Have students complete the exercise.

3. Ask individual students to read their matches. Encourage discussion.

Expansion/Homework

Write the famous sentence by Noam Chomsky on the board: *Colorless green ideas sleep furiously.* Is the sentence correct? Does it make sense? Why or why not? Briefly discuss the relationship between grammar and meaning with the class.

VOCABULARY EXPANSION: Suffixes

1. Have students write the root/base word and the suffix for these vocabulary words:

successful	success	ful
agreement	agree	ment
production	product	tion/ion

2. Have students brainstorm examples of other words that use these suffixes and then check the meaning of the suffixes in a dictionary.

For example: -ful   careful, successful, powerful, harmful, helpful

-ment   advertisement, announcement, government, measurement

-tion   attention, detention, education, subtraction

Students can then add the suffixes to the section designated in their personal dictionary.

✪ CREATE

Suggested Time: 20 minutes

1. Review the words in the box and make sure their meaning is clear.

2. Have students write a paragraph explaining different views on climate change using at least five words from the box. Allow students to express their own opinions as well as those from the readings, but insist that the new vocabulary be used.

3. Divide the class into small groups. Have students exchange paragraphs and correct each other's work. Move around the room and provide assistance where necessary.

4. If time allows, invite a few students to read their paragraphs to the class.

 Go to www.mynorthstarlab.com for additional *Vocabulary* practice.

✪✪ B GRAMMAR: Future Possibility: *May, Might, Could*

Go to www.mynorthstarlab.com for *Grammar Chart* and *Exercise 2*.

◖ SKILLS

Use modals to express future possibility.

Suggested Time: 20 minutes

1. Ask a student to read the paragraph in **Exercise 1** to the class. Individually, have students underline the target words.

2. Go over the information in the grammar chart with the class. Call on individual students to read the examples. Pay particular attention to the rules for forming questions, as this is a difficult concept for many students.

3. Have students complete **Exercise 2** individually. Then go over the answers with the class. Remember that there can be more than one answer to some of the questions.

4. Go over the instructions for **Exercise 3** with the class. Have students write 3–5 questions to ask their partner. Then divide the class into pairs and have students take turns asking and answering each other's questions using *may, might,* and *could.* Move around the classroom and listen to the questions and answers, offering help or correction where appropriate.

Expansion/Homework

For further practice, offer exercises from *Focus on Grammar 3,* 3rd Edition or Azar's *Fundamentals of English Grammar,* 3rd Edition. See the Grammar Book References on page 219 of the student book for specific units and chapters.

 Go to www.mynorthstarlab.com for additional *Grammar* practice.

C WRITING

If you wish to assign a different writing task than the one in this section, see page 183. The Alternative Writing Topics can also be assigned as additional writing topics for homework. The alternative topics relate to the theme of the unit, but may not target the same grammar or rhetorical structures taught in the unit.

◀ SKILLS

Use a causal chain to express relationships between causes and effects; use transitions to express cause and effect; integrate the concepts, vocabulary, grammar, and rhetorical structures from the unit to plan, develop, and write a cause-and-effect essay.

✪✪✪ PREPARE TO WRITE: Using a Causal Chain

Suggested Time: 10 minutes

1. Explain to students that as a culminating activity, they will write a cause-and-effect essay. Go over the information in the task box with the class.

2. Remind students of the causal chain introduced in the reading section of the unit and have them study the causal chain in **Exercise 1**. Explain that the causal chain shows how one cause leads to one or more effects and the arrows in the chain are a good way to illustrate that.

3. Read the instructions for **Exercise 2** with the class. Ask students to think of some causes and effects they want to write about in their essays and then to draw a causal chain. Move around the room and provide assistance where necessary.

Expansion/Homework

Some students may choose a different way to organize their thoughts such as a vertical flowchart or a non-linear mind map. Allow students to choose alternatives that best meet their learning styles.

✿✿✿ WRITE: A Cause-and-Effect Essay

Suggested Time: 35 minutes

1. Read aloud the brief introduction to a cause-and-effect essay. Then have students read the essay in **Exercise 1** and complete the activity that follows. Go over the answers with the class and write the topic sentence on the board. Invite individual students to the front of the class to draw cause-and-effect maps for questions 2–4. Encourage debate.

2. Go over the instructions for **Exercise 2** and have students return to their own causal chains and add details to support their causes and effects.

3. Go over the instructions for **Exercise 3** with the class. Make sure students understand the task. Then have students use their causal chains to write a first draft of their essays. Move around the room and provide assistance if necessary. You can also assign writing the first draft as homework.

Expansion/Homework

Be aware that cause-and-effect is a way of thinking that is not found in every culture. This linear approach can be difficult for students to comprehend and needs time to practice. Choose additional topics and have students practice building causal chains.

 Link to *NorthStar: Listening and Speaking 3*

If students are also using the companion text, allow them to use information and graphs from Unit 9 of the *Listening and Speaking* strand in their essays.

✿✿✿ REVISE: Using Cause-and-Effect Transitions

Suggested Time: 20 minutes

1. Ask students to read the sentences in **Exercise 1**. Pause after each sentence and ask students to explain the meaning of the boldfaced words. Students should be familiar with these words. Ask them if the boldfaced words express a cause or an effect.

2. Read the explanation in the box aloud to the class and answer any question students may have.

3. Have students complete **Exercise 2**. First have them read through the entire text before completing the blanks. Remind them to add commas where necessary. Then call on individual students to read the completed paragraphs. Correct any mistakes.

4. Have students read the instructions for **Exercise 3** and then return to their own essays and add cause-and-effect transitions where appropriate to give their arguments more clarity.

Expansion/Homework

For additional practice, have students create a causal chain based on the report in Exercise 2.

✪✪✪ EDIT: Writing the Final Draft

Suggested Time: 25 minutes

Have students write the final draft of their essays. Encourage them to use language and grammar from the unit. Make sure they go through the checklist before submitting their final drafts. Collect the essays and correct them before the next class.

Expansion/Homework

Explain to students that many people believe that everything we do has an effect on something, no matter how small that effect may be. Ask students if they agree with this statement and think about their own daily lives. Can they establish cause-and-effect relationships for their daily actions, or can they find actions that have no effect at all? Have students write a short essay on this subject or organize a class discussion.

 Go to www.mynorthstarlab.com for *Writing the Final Draft*.

✪ ALTERNATIVE WRITING TOPICS

These topics give students an alternative opportunity to explore and write about issues related to the unit theme.

✪ RESEARCH TOPICS

Suggested Time: 20 minutes in class

1. Have students turn to page 215. Review the instructions for the activity with the class. Tell students to choose one topic from the list and use a search engine or library materials to look for information that provides information about the topic.

2. Have students answer the questions in Step 2. Encourage them to write any additional information they might find.

3. Have students write a report about their findings. Remind them to use visual aids with their reports. Then have students present their reports to the class or in small groups.

 Go to www.mynorthstarlab.com for *Student Writing Models, Integrated Task, Video Activity, Internet Activity,* and *Unit 9 Achievement Test*.

UNIT 10
Crime and Punishment

OVERVIEW

Theme: Punishment

This unit focuses on the capital punishment debate. Students are given an opportunity to explore opinions for and against capital punishment and express their own opinions about the issue in discussion and writing.

Reading One: *Two Points of View* is a set of two editorials: one in favor of capital punishment and one against it.

Reading Two: *Charts* is a collection of charts and graphs presenting statistics on the death penalty.

Critical Thinking

Interpret a photograph
Distinguish arguments for and against capital punishment
Infer word meaning from context

Interpret bar graphs and pie charts
Classify information
Draw conclusions

Reading

Make predictions
Identify supporting ideas in an argument
Relate supporting details to main ideas

Express opinions about capital punishment
Read graphs and charts
Distinguish between fact and opinion

Writing

Write an opinion paragraph
Support opinions with facts and data
Write an outline for a debate
List ideas

Use sentence variety
Analyze compound sentences
Write a persuasive essay

Vocabulary	Grammar
Use context clues to find meaning Define words Identify abstract nouns Practice appropriate word usage	Present perfect and present perfect progressive

MyNorthStarLab Readiness Check, Background and Vocabulary, Readings One and Two, Notetaking and Academic Skills Practice, Vocabulary and Grammar, Writing the Final Draft, Achievement Test	***NorthStar: Listening and Speaking 3*** Unit 10 explores the legal and social aspects of corporal punishment.

FOCUS ON THE TOPIC

◖ SKILLS

Predict the content of the unit; share opinions about capital punishment; infer meaning of new vocabulary from context.

❖❖❖ A PREDICT

Suggested Time: 10 minutes

1. Have students look at the photograph and guess what it shows. If students don't know, explain that the photograph shows an execution bed used by prisons to administer the death penalty. Make sure you are very careful with this topic. It might be extremely upsetting for some students to discuss it. Be sensitive to students' feelings and opinions.

2. Introduce the word *execution* and have students circle the remaining words in the box that relate to capital punishment. Go over the word selections with the class. Accept all answers from students provided they can explain the word relationship.

❖❖ B SHARE INFORMATION

Suggested Time: 15 minutes

1. Read the questions together, and then divide students into small groups. To facilitate cooperative learning, appoint a discussion leader and information recorder for each group. Have groups discuss the questions. Move around the room and provide vocabulary as needed.

2. Call on groups to share their answers and opinions with the class. Be sensitive to students' attitudes; some may feel embarrassed about their governments' policies, so be careful not to focus on a particular country unless students seem willing to volunteer information.

Expansion/Homework
To help students discuss item 3, it might be helpful to draw a T-chart on the board or on a transparency to help them organize their ideas. One side of the chart can be used to list ideas under the rubric "fair," while the other side can be used to list ideas under the rubric "unfair."

 **C** BACKGROUND AND VOCABULARY

📁 Go to www.mynorthstarlab.com for *Background and Vocabulary.*

Suggested Time: 20 minutes

1. Tell students to read the facts about capital punishment in **Exercise 1** without worrying about new vocabulary items. Then have them read the text again attempting to understand the boldfaced words. Then ask students if they knew any of the facts or whether any of the facts surprised them.

2. Have students complete **Exercise 2**, matching words with their definitions.

3. Go over the answers as a class and provide additional examples for vocabulary words that remain unclear.

📁 Go to www.mynorthstarlab.com for additional *Background and Vocabulary* practice.

②FOCUS ON READING

◖SKILLS

Predict opinions; identify supporting ideas in an argument; relate supporting details to main ideas; infer opinions based on the information in the reading; express opinions about capital punishment in a paragraph; read and interpret charts and graphs.

A READING ONE: Two Points of View

📁 Go to www.mynorthstarlab.com to read and listen to *Two Points of View.*

Suggested Time: 30 minutes

Reading One consists of two editorials that present both sides of the capital punishment debate. The readings give students an opportunity to explore opinions for and against capital punishment in the context of newspaper articles.

1. Have students read the introduction and explain that an editorial is a type of newspaper article that is not neutral, but expresses the writer's opinion on a topic.

2. Divide the class into small groups and have students discuss what they expect each editorial to contain. Have one student take notes on the discussion. Call on groups to read their predictions to the class. Affirm each prediction as a possibility.

3. Have students read the editorials. Move around the room and explain any unfamiliar vocabulary. The reading can be assigned as homework or lab work using MyNorthStarLab. You can also choose to play the recording of the reading and have students listen as they read.

READING STRATEGY: Persuasive Writing

1. To help students with the persuasive aspects of this reading selection, give them a controversial statement that is close to their experience (for example, Students should have more homework; Students should be required to do a year of community service after graduation; Young people under 21 should not be allowed to drive).

2. Have students work in small groups to take a position for each of these, or similar statements and write three reasons in support of their opinion. Provide large chart paper for presentations and have students share their thesis statement and three reasons with the class.

✪✪✪ READ FOR MAIN IDEAS

Suggested Time: 10 minutes

Copy Opinions A and B onto the board. Then have students silently read the numbered statements and match them to the correct opinion. Go over the answers with the class and ask students to identify where the information can be found in the two editorials. If there is time, invite students to share their own ideas related to the two opinions.

REACHING ALL STUDENTS: Read for Main Ideas

• **Less Proficient:** Have students list eight reasons that support the writer's argument that capital punishment is wrong.	• **More Proficient:** Suggest that students argue for and against capital punishment by listing five reasons in support of each position.

✪✪✪ READ FOR DETAILS

Suggested Time: 15 minutes

1. Go over the instructions with the class and make sure students understand the task. They must understand that each detail offers specific information that relates to one of the more general main ideas.

2. If necessary, have students read the editorials again. Then have students match details to the main ideas in the previous exercise. Tell students to refer back to the text if they need to. Go over the answers with the class. If students have difficulty, complete the exercise as a class.

Expansion/Homework

Point out that this exercise is also a step in building an outline for an essay. If time allows, have students take the main points and details and arrange them in outlines for each editorial. Students may also want to add their own main ideas and details to support either opinion.

✪✪✪ MAKE INFERENCES

Suggested Time: 15 minutes

1. Focus students on the chart and give them a few minutes to read the quotes.

2. Have students refer back to the two editorials and find passages to refute the quotes in the chart. Have students compare their selections with a partner's. Then invite individual students to share their selections with the class. If there are disagreements, have students discuss their answers and support their opinions.

 Link to *NorthStar: Listening and Speaking 3*

If students are also using the companion text, have them make inferences about the parents and experts who spoke in Listening One. Ask students to consider the following questions: *What does a parent who supports spanking believe about children? What does a parent who opposes spanking believe about children? What kind of person chooses to become an expert on raising children?* Encourage students to focus on attitudes and beliefs in their answers.

✪✪✪ EXPRESS OPINIONS

Suggested Time: 15 minutes

1. Read the instructions and the statements with the class. Give students a minute to decide which editorial they agree with.

2. Using information from Make Inferences, have students write a brief paragraph expressing their position on capital punishment.

3. Divide the class into pairs and have students exchange paragraphs, read each other's opinions, and discuss.

CRITICAL THINKING

Give students the following questions for discussion in small groups before discussing as a whole class:

1. Why do you think it costs more to execute a prisoner than to keep them in prison for life?

   Answers will vary, but might include the cost of appeals, trials, and housing on death row. Ask students to support their speculations with their own knowledge.

2. Do you think people who are in prison can experience a reasonably good life?

   Answers will vary, but students should be able to support their opinions with information from the text, or from their own knowledge.

3. Mistakes are made in the justice system and innocent people are executed. Is this a good reason to abolish the death penalty?

   Answers will vary, but students should be able to support their opinions with information from the text or from their own knowledge.

4. Why do you think the poor and minorities get the death penalty more than whites?

   Answers will vary, but students should be able to support their opinions with information from the text, or from their own knowledge.

✪✪✪ B READING TWO: Charts

📁 Go to www.mynorthstarlab.com to read and listen to *Charts*.

Suggested Time: 25 minutes

Reading Two is a set of bar graphs and pie charts that present information and facts about the death penalty. It extends the topic of capital punishment and gives students an opportunity to practice reading and interpreting statistical information.

1. Explain to students that the charts they are going to read and analyze provide valuable data on the controversial subject of capital punishment.

2. Divide the class into pairs and have each pair read the graphs and answer the questions. Point out that it is important not only to read data, but also to understand when, where, and by whom it was collected.

3. Go over the answers to the questions with the class. Ask the students if any of the information surprised them. If so, why?

Expansion/Homework
Have each pair write a short paragraph summarizing the information in one of the charts.

✪✪✪ C INTEGRATE READINGS ONE AND TWO

◀ SKILLS

Distinguish between facts and opinions; create an outline for a debate by synthesizing information from the readings.

STEP 1: Organize   Suggested Time: 10 minutes

1. Elicit the distinction between a fact and an opinion from students. Ask for examples of each in a sentence.

2. Have students read the statements and mark them as either fact or opinion.

3. Go over the answers with the class. Encourage debate and challenge students to provide specific examples from the reading to support their claims.

STEP 2: Synthesize   Suggested Time: 15 minutes

1. Explain to students that opinions have more power when they are supported by facts and other concrete information, especially in a formal academic discussion or debate.

2. Read the instructions with the class and focus students on the debate outlines. Invite a student to read the first two points of the outline for debate team X.

3. Have students complete the outlines with opinions and facts from Step 1. Then have students form small groups and compare their outlines.

Expansion/Homework
Divide the class into two groups, one pro and one con, and conduct a debate using the completed outlines. You can also allow students to add their own opinions and facts to support their positions. Be sure that each student in a group presents at least one point. If you have a large class, break the class up into multiple debates.

 Go to www.mynorthstarlab.com for *Notetaking* and *Academic Skills Practice*.

A VOCABULARY

◖ SKILLS

Review vocabulary from Readings One and Two; apply vocabulary learned in the unit to a new context—an essay; identify abstract nouns and match them to examples; identify synonyms; choose language to strengthen or soften an argument; use new vocabulary creatively to write a paragraph expressing opinions on the future of punishment for murder.

✪ REVIEW   Suggested Time: 15 minutes

 Go to www.mynorthstarlab.com for *Review*.

1. Have students read through the essay once. Then have them go through the essay paragraph by paragraph and fill in the gaps with the appropriate word from the box.

2. Call on students to take turns reading one paragraph each. Encourage the rest of the class to listen closely and correct any mistakes.

✪✪ EXPAND   Suggested Time: 25 minutes

1. Go over the definition of abstract nouns with the class. To check students' understanding of the concept, elicit some examples of abstract nouns from them.

2. Have students complete **Exercise 1**. Go over the answers with the class.

3. Go over the instructions for **Exercise 2** and have students complete the task. Invite students to share their answers. Encourage classmates to listen closely and correct mistakes.

4. Go over the instructions for **Exercise 3** with the class. Be sure students understand the task. Then have students complete the exercise. Discuss the answers with the class.

Expansion/Homework
To give students more opportunities to work with synonyms, have them work in pairs to generate lists of synonyms for each underlined word in Exercise 3. For example, in item 7 they might think of *damage, harm, ruin* as synonyms for *hurt*. Discuss the differences in meaning that occur when synonyms are used.

VOCABULARY EXPANSION: Vocabulary Story

1. Using a vocabulary story helps students to encode it into long-term memory. This strategy is fun for students because it employs right-brain creativity with left brain vocabulary study.

2. Tell students they are going to work with their partner to create a story a few paragraphs in length, which will use at least eight of the following vocabulary words: *murderer, cruel, justice, respect, right, citizenship, execution, society, forgiveness, innocent, guilty, violent, revenge.* Students should first work together to create their story verbally, and then put it in writing. Allow time for students to read their finished story to the class.

✪ CREATE   **Suggested Time: 20 minutes**

1. Go over the instructions and the questions with the class and give students a few minutes to make notes. Then have them write a short persuasive paragraph outlining their position on the future of punishment for murderers. Make sure they use at least five words from the list.

2. Call on individual students to read their paragraphs for the class. Encourage class discussion.

Expansion/Homework
This activity can also be done for homework. Collect the paragraphs, correct them, and return them the following class. Invite individual students to read their paragraphs. Encourage class discussion.

Go to www.mynorthstarlab.com for additional *Vocabulary* practice.

✷✷ Ⓑ GRAMMAR: Present Perfect and Present Perfect Progressive

Go to www.mynorthstarlab.com for *Grammar Chart* and *Exercise 2*.

❰ SKILLS

Understand and contrast the uses of the present perfect and present perfect progressive tenses.

Suggested Time: 20 minutes

1. Ask students to silently read the paragraphs in **Exercise 1**. As a class, discuss the similarities and differences between the tenses.

2. Review the grammar chart with the class. Ask students to read the explanations and examples. Allow time for any questions or comments.

3. Have students complete **Exercise 2**. Call on students to read their answers. Ask them to point out which grammar rule from the chart supports their choice.

4. Refer students back to the charts in Reading Two on pages 192–194 and make complete sentences using the present perfect and present perfect progressive. Invite students to read their sentences to the class. Encourage the class to listen closely and suggest corrections if they identify errors.

Expansion/Homework

For further practice, offer exercises from *Focus on Grammar 3*, 3rd Edition or Azar's *Fundamentals of English Grammar*, 3rd Edition. See the Grammar Book References on page 219 of the student book for specific units and chapters.

 Go to www.mynorthstarlab.com for additional *Grammar* practice.

C WRITING

If you wish to assign a different writing task than the one in this section, see page 210. The Alternative Writing Topics can also be assigned as additional writing topics for homework. The alternative topics relate to the theme of the unit, but may not target the same grammar or rhetorical structures taught in the unit.

◖ SKILLS

List reasons for and against capital punishment; use sentence variety; complete an outline; integrate the concepts, vocabulary, grammar, and rhetorical structures from the unit to write a persuasive essay.

✵✵✵ PREPARE TO WRITE: Listing

Suggested Time: 10 minutes

1. Explain to students that as a culminating activity, they will write a persuasive essay. Go over the information in the task box with the class.

2. Individually, have students brainstorm reasons for and against capital punishment. The ideas can be their own or from the readings. They should list ideas regardless of their personal opinions.

3. Next, have students choose which side of the capital punishment debate to support and put a check next to all the points they agree with from the list they just created. Allow students to organize their ideas in graphic organizers or any way that they feel comfortable with.

✪✪✪ WRITE: A Persuasive Essay

Suggested Time: 35 minutes

1. Write the word *persuade* on the board. Elicit the meaning of the word from students (*convince, influence*). Ask students what a persuasive essay might be. Then have a student read the information about persuasive essays to the class.

2. Have students read the essay in **Exercise 1** and discuss the questions in small groups. Go over the answers as a class.

3. Go over the instructions in **Exercise 2** and have students choose a position to support. Move around the room and ask questions and provide advice where appropriate.

4. Have students plan their essay by completing the outline in **Exercise 3**. Spot-check the outlines, paying particular attention to thesis, topic sentences, and conclusion.

5. Have students complete **Exercise 4** and write a first draft of their essays. You can also assign writing the first draft as homework.

 Link to *NorthStar: Listening and Speaking 3*

If the death penalty debate is too upsetting to students, allow them to write a persuasive essay about corporal punishment. Another interesting option is to explore how the experience with corporal punishment in childhood influences our attitudes and inclination towards violence when we are adults.

✪✪✪ REVISE: Using Sentence Variety

Suggested Time: 25 minutes

1. Invite a student to read the paragraph in **Exercise 1**. Ask students if they can identify similarities and differences between the sentences.

2. Discuss sentence variety and go over the examples in the chart. Offer additional explanations and examples if necessary.

3. Have students complete **Exercise 2**. Encourage them to use coordinating and subordinating conjunctions as well as subject pronouns. Then divide the class into pairs and have students edit each other's work. Move around the room and offer assistance where appropriate.

4. Focus students on the letter in **Exercise 3**. Explain that they will now act as editors and must make the letter more interesting by using a better variety of sentences. Have students rewrite the letter. Then invite individual students to read their rewritten letters to the class. Encourage the rest of the class to listen carefully and note any mistakes they might hear.

5. Go over the instructions for **Exercise 4** and have students return to their first drafts and edit them with an eye to sentence variety.

✪✪✪ EDIT: Writing the Final Draft

Suggested Time: 25 minutes

Have students write the final draft of their paragraphs. Encourage them to use language and grammar from the unit. Make sure they go through the checklist before submitting their final drafts. Collect the paragraphs and correct them before the next class.

 Go to www.mynorthstarlab.com for *Writing the Final Draft*.

✪ ALTERNATIVE WRITING TOPICS

These topics give students an alternative opportunity to explore and write about issues related to the unit theme.

✪ RESEARCH TOPICS

Suggested Time: 20 minutes in class

1. Have students turn to page 216. Review the instructions for the activity with the class. Tell students to choose one country from the list and do library research about death penalty laws in that country. Tell students they can also use a search engine to look for information that provides information about the topic. Remind students to answer the questions in their reports. You can also brainstorm other questions that can be added to the list.

2. After students complete their research, have them present their findings in small groups. Then have them write a report based on the findings and present it to the class.

 Go to www.mynorthstarlab.com for *Student Writing Models, Integrated Task, Video Activity, Internet Activity,* and *Unit 10 Achievement Test.*

Student Book Answer Key

UNIT I

IC BACKGROUND AND VOCABULARY, pages 2–3

2. Global
3. goal
4. campaigns
5. fail
6. message
7. markets
8. convince
9. succeed
10. competition

READ FOR MAIN IDEAS, page 5

Answers will vary. Suggested answers:

1. Jacko is an Australian football player who appeared in the battery ads. His failure in the United States campaign shows that advertisers need to change their campaigns when they advertise in different countries.
2. The translation could be wrong. A wrong translation may send the wrong message.
3. The global advertisers must pay attention to different communication styles as well as different laws and customs.
4. A company should do this because people in different countries have different likes and dislikes.

READ FOR DETAILS, pages 5–6

2. c
3. b
4. b
5. c
6. d
7. d
8. b

MAKE INFERENCES, pages 6–7

2. c; paragraph 4
3. a; paragraph 4
4. b; paragraph 5
5. c; paragraph 3

STEP I: Organize, pages 9–10

2. d
3. a
4. e
5. b

STEP 2: Synthesize, page 10

1. global advertising
2. illegal
3. commercial advertiser
4. product preferences
5. convince
6. *vatrushka*
7. customs
8. difficult

REVIEW, page 11

2. b
3. c
4. b
5. d
6. d
7. c
8. a
9. d
10. b

EXPAND

1, page 12

2. d
3. b
4. e
5. a

2, page 12

1. impression
2. impressive
3. impress

3B GRAMMAR

2, pages 13–14

2. is increasing
3. fail
4. consider
5. are writing
6. make
7. like
8. is growing

3, page 14

Answers will vary. The correct tense should be used:

1. present progressive
2. simple present
3. present progressive
4. simple present

WRITE

2, page 16

1. D3
2. D1
3. D2
4. TS
5. CS

REVISE

1, page 16

Answer c needs to be crossed out.

2, page 17

Topic sentence:

I recently saw a very effective advertisement for Pepsi-Cola on television.

The following sentences need to be crossed out:

1. In fact, she looks just like my friend's grandmother.
2. Mysterious ads are not common on TV.
3. Finally, the ad is not respectful of the elderly.
4. Nowadays, some people are making fun of the elderly.
5. I don't like this.

UNIT 2

IC BACKGROUND AND VOCABULARY

2, page 21

1. a
2. b
3. b
4. a
5. a
6. b
7. b
8. a

READ FOR MAIN IDEAS, page 24

a. 3
b. 5
c. 6
e. 2
f. 4

READ FOR DETAILS, page 24

2. k
3. e
4. i
5. c
6. a
7. g
8. b
9. d
10. h
11. f

MAKE INFERENCES, pages 24–25

1. b
2. a
3. b
4. b
5. a

2B READING TWO

2, page 26

1. F   2. F   3. T   4. F   5. T

STEP I: Organize, page 27

R1: Financial consequences: d, j
R1: Emotional and psychological consequences: c, f, i
R2: Financial consequences: g, h, k
R2 Emotional and psychological consequences: b, e, l

REVIEW, pages 28–30

2. impersonate   6. weary   10. honesty
3. fake   7. suspicious   11. motive
4. astonishing   8. fishy   12. con man
5. impressed   9. deception

EXPAND

1, page 30

Noun	Verb	Adjective	Adverb
1. deception	deceive	deceptive	deceptively
2. duplicate	duplicate	duplicate	x
3. fakery	fake	fake	x
4. fraud	x	fraudulent	fraudulently
5. honesty	x	honest	honestly
6. impersonation	impersonate	x	x
7. motive	motivate	motivated	x

2, page 30

2. I had a bad experience with a man who practiced fraudulent medicine.
3. Making money motivated him.
4. Not many people understood that he was a fake.
5. I wasn't the only person that he deceived.
6. He wasn't a real doctor, but his impersonation was good.
7. He had made a duplicate of someone else's medical license.

3B GRAMMAR

2, pages 32–33

2. my neighbors were relaxing at home on Sunday.
3. my neighbors answered their door.
4. they took the checks to the bank.
5. they were adding the "H"; they added the "H."
6. a bank clerk finally became suspicious of what they were doing.
7. , the police arrested the two men.
8. I was watching the news on TV.

REVISE

1, page 35

1. My sister wasted a lot of money on a fraudulent weight loss product.
2. I had a bad experience with a dentist who promised to make my teeth look white.

2, page 36

1. b   2. c   3. a

3, pages 36–37

Answers will vary. Suggested answers:

1. Once, I wasted a lot of time buying face cream that didn't work.
2. I made a big mistake when I bought fraudulent language CDs.
3. My uncle had an embarrassing experience with a fraudulent hair product.

UNIT 3

IC BACKGROUND AND VOCABULARY, pages 40–41

2. b   5. a   8. a   11. b
3. a   6. b   9. a   12. a
4. b   7. a   10. b

READ FOR MAIN IDEAS, page 44

1. F   2. T   3. F   4. F   5. F   6. T

READ FOR DETAILS, page 44

1. He landed the 900.
2. 13 years
3. when he was 10 years old
4. at the Oasis Skate Park
5. He was considered a freak and all the jocks picked on him. Also, he couldn't sit still in class.
6. his son

MAKE INFERENCES, pages 44–45

1, 3, 4, 5, 7, 8

2B READING TWO

2, page 46

1. a   2. b   3. a   4. b   5. a

STEP I: Organize, page 47

Tony Hawk: Obsession leads to success
                   Family is supportive
Both: Desire to be the best
                   Obsession helps to escape pain
                   Competitive
                   Dedicated

Ashley Lindermann: Life of pressure
Obsession leads to anorexia
World seems scary
Need to feel in control
Family adds pressure

REVIEW, pages 48–49

1. achieved	5. control	8. escape
2. athlete	6. focus	9. hooked on
3. obsessed	7. awesome	10. benefit
4. intense		

EXPAND, page 50

Noun	Verb	Adjective	Adverb
1. achievement	achieve	achieved	x
2. athlete	x	athletic	athletically
3. benefit	benefit	beneficial	beneficially
4. concentration	concentrate	concentrated	x
5. controversy	x	controversial	x
6. energy	energize	energetic	energetically
7. focus	focus	focused	x
8. intensity	intensify	intense	intensely
9. mentality	x	mental	mentally
10. obsession	obsess	obsessive	obsessively
11. perfectionist	perfect	perfect	perfectly
12. performance; performer	perform	performing	x
13. physicality	x	physical	physically
14. pressure	pressure	pressured	x
15. qualification	qualify	qualifying	x

3B GRAMMAR

2, page 52

1. could	6. could
2. be able to	7. be able to
3. can't	8. be able to
4. wasn't able to / couldn't	9. Could
5. could	

WRITE

1, page 54

B.
2. b	4. b	6. e	8. c	10. e
3. b	5. b	7. c	9. c	11. c, d

REVISE

1, page 56

According to ANRED, Anorexia Nervosa and Related Eating Disorders, an organization that provides information about eating disorders, eating disorders continue to be on the rise among athletes, especially in sports that emphasize being thin. Sports such as gymnastics, figure skating, dancing, and synchronized swimming have a higher percentage of athletes with eating disorders. According to an American College of Sports Medicine study, eating disorders affected 62% of the females in these sports. Cathy Rigby, a 1972 Olympic gymnast, has admitted she struggled with anorexia for 12 years. Anorexia nervosa, an eating disorder in which the person diets so much that they become too thin, affects about 1% of female adolescents in the United States. Bulimia nervosa, an eating disorder in which the person diets, becomes hungry, overeats, and then vomits to get rid of the food, affects about 4% of college-aged women. If you want more information, contact the NEDIC, National Eating Disorder Information Center.

UNIT 4

IC BACKGROUND AND VOCABULARY

2, page 61

1. c	3. g	5. d	7. f	9. a
2. i	4. b	6. h	8. e	

2A READING ONE, page 62

1. They decorated her room in pink and white. They told their relatives and friends they were having a girl.
2. They sent gifts that included pink dresses and dolls.
3. *Answers will vary.*

READ FOR MAIN IDEAS, page 64

2. T
3. T
4. F: Gender differences can be seen in the ways that children use language when they play.
5. F: Differences in communication between males and females are different in all cultures.
6. F: Boys gain status by showing their knowledge about sports and news.
7. T
8. F: Women usually talk more about other people than men do.

READ FOR DETAILS, page 65

Paragraph

2.	a	1
3.	b	2
4.	b	4
5.	a	5
6.	c	7
7.	a	9
8.	c	10
9.	b	11

MAKE INFERENCES, page 66

Paragraph

1.	c	3
2.	b	1, 2
3.	c	6
4.	c	4, 5
5.	a	10

2B READING TWO

2, page 68

Answers will vary. Suggested answers:

1. These words might make women feel less important than men.
2. police officer, firefighter, mail carrier
3. They changed as a result of the women's movement.
4. Women use more words to describe colors. Women use adjectives that men don't use such as *lovely, cute, and adorable.*

STEP 1: Organize, pages 68–69

Males	Females
2. commands	3. gossip
4. to solve	5. strangers
6. doing things	7. tag questions
8. purple	9. lovely, cute, adorable
10. ka	10. no

REVIEW, pages 70–71

1.	emphasize	6.	fairly
2.	masculine	7.	occupation
3.	influence	8.	status
4.	compete	9.	reflect
5.	feminine	10.	women's movement

EXPAND, pages 71–72

1. d   2. f   3. b   4. e   5. c   6. a

3B GRAMMAR

2, page 73

1.	as fluently as	4.	as skillfully as
2.	more rapidly than	5.	more carefully than
3.	more slowly than	6.	less perfectly than

REVISE

3, page 76

Answers will vary. Suggested answers:

1. Tommy enjoys playing with a large group of boys. On the other hand, Joy doesn't like it when new girls join her friends.
2. Unlike girls, boys often compete with one another for leadership. Girls are not usually interested in competing with each other.
3. Boys often gain status through playing sports, in contrast to girls, who often gain status through gossip.
4. Men usually want to use a map to find directions. Women, on the other hand, usually want to ask a stranger for directions.
5. My English class is very informal. However, the office where I work is very formal.
6. In contrast to speaking English to people I know well, speaking English to strangers is sometimes difficult.

UNIT 5

READ FOR MAIN IDEAS, page 83

3, 1, 2

READ FOR DETAILS

1, page 84

I. A. the oldest
   B. view
   C. harsh
II. A. research projects
   B. plants and animals
   C. animal and plant life

2, page 84

2. The writer wants Antarctica to be closed to tourists.
3. Psychologists study how people behave when they live and work together in such a remote location.
4. Oil spills in Antarctica have killed penguins and destroyed a five-year scientific project.
5. Tour companies may not be concerned about the environment of Antarctica.
6. If we don't protect Antarctica from tourism, there may be serious consequences for us all.
7. We know from past experience that when things get unbalanced, harmful changes can occur.

MAKE INFERENCES, page 85

1. L	3. L	5. U
2. L	4. U	

STEP 1: Organize, page 88

Answers may vary. Suggested answers:

Opinions of the Scientist:

3. Tourists take scientists away from their research, can damage scientific projects, and hurt the environment.

Opinions of the Tourist:

2. Tourists can follow rules made by scientists.
4. Tourists are interested in learning about Antarctica.

REVIEW, page 89

Answers will vary. Suggested answers:

coastal: sunlight, temperature, research, beauty
fragile: environment, beauty, landscape, glaciers
frozen: icebergs, environment, landscape, continent
harsh: effect, sunlight, temperature, environment, beauty, landscape consequences, continent
natural: effect, sunlight, temperature, environment, beauty, landscape
remote: icebergs, environment, glaciers
scientific: research
vast: research, environment, beauty, landscape, continent, glaciers, icebergs

EXPAND, page 90

2. a; C / E	5. b; C / E	8. b; S
3. b; S	6. b; S	9. a; C / E
4. a; A	7. b; S	10. a; S

3B GRAMMAR

2, page 92

2. Even though I understand why tourists want to see Antarctica, they shouldn't be allowed to visit.
3. Because the earth's temperature is rising, meteorologists are worried.
4. Antarctica's unique environment is in danger because there is no government in Antarctica to help preserve it.
5. Even though tourists enjoy the beauty of Antarctica, they sometimes damage the environment.
6. Even though scientists are interested in protecting Antarctica's natural environment, tour companies are not.
7. We had an amazing time on this remote continent even though it was difficult to travel in such a harsh environment.
8. Because Antarctica is unbelievably scenic, tourists recommend it to their friends.

WRITE

1, page 94

1. And even though I can appreciate their desire to experience this vast and beautiful landscape, I feel Antarctica should be closed to tourists.
2. **Paragraph 2:** Because Antarctica is the center of important scientific research, it must be preserved for this purpose.
   Paragraph 3: When tourist groups come here, they take us away from our research.
   Paragraph 4: The need to protect Antarctica from tourists becomes even greater when we consider the fact that there is no government here.
3. **Paragraph 2:** examples
   Paragraph 3: reasons
   Paragraph 4: explanation
4. Clearly, Antarctica should remain a place for careful and controlled scientific research.

REVISE

2, page 96

1. c   2. a   3. b

UNIT 6

1C BACKGROUND AND VOCABULARY

2, page 101

1. b	3. h	5. d	7. l	9. c	11. i
2. f	4. a	6. j	8. e	10. g	12. k

READ FOR MAIN IDEAS, page 104

Answers may vary. Suggested answers:

1. Gregor has become an insect.
2. His family is frightened when they see Gregor.
3. Only his sister takes care of him, and she eventually stops.
4. He dies in his room as he thinks about his family.
5. His family feels relieved when he dies.

READ FOR DETAILS, page 105

2. Gregor panicked and said, "No, no, I will come out immediately."
3. He began to back out of the room to leave, and Gregor realized he couldn't let him go.
4. He slid under the couch and slept there until morning.
5. The next morning, Gregor's sister looked in and was surprised to see that he hadn't eating a thing.
6. The first few didn't hurt him, but then one pierced his body, and he felt terrible pain.
7. His sister also began to care less and less about feeding him and cleaning his room.
8. "We must find a way to get rid of this thing."

MAKE INFERENCES, page 106

1. T: "Gregor, are you all right? Do you need anything?" *p 2*
2. F
3. T: At the sight of him, the manager screamed, his mother fainted, and his father wept. *p 5*
4. T: The family now left his door to the dining room open for two hours every night after dinner, and he could listen to their conversation. He really loved this. *p 16*
5. T: Grete became very upset. "Momma, Poppa," she said, "This cannot go on. We must find a way to get rid of this thing. It is destroying our lives." *p 10*

2B READING TWO

2, page 107

Answers will vary. Suggested answers:

1. The critic thinks this story is funny because of how Gregor learns to move his insect legs and body. It is sad because his family stops loving him when he becomes disgusting.
2. It means *vermin*. It can mean a person who is rough and disgusting. Gregor is like a vermin—a parasite to his family, having no responsibility and being a burden.

STEP 1: Organize, page 108

Answers will vary. Suggested answers:

1. Lying on his back, he could see his large brown belly and thin legs.

   He tried to turn over onto his side, but every time he tried, he would roll onto his back again.

   When he answered her, he was surprised to hear his voice; it sounded so high.

   His thin little legs seemed useless, just moving and moving in the air, not helping him at all.

   He began rocking back and forth, stronger and more intensely, and finally threw himself onto the floor, hitting his head as he fell.

2. His mother rushed over to his father to beg him not to kill Gregor, as Gregor slowly crawled back to his room.

   Grete became very upset. "Momma, Poppa," she said, "This cannot go on. We must find a way to get rid of this thing. It is destroying our lives."

3. "Yes, mother. I'm getting up now."
4. One morning, Gregor Samsa woke up from a bad dream and realized he was some kind of terrible insect.
5. He hated his job, but he had to do it to support his father, mother, and sister because his father no longer worked.

6. One morning, Gregor Samsa woke up from a bad dream and realized he was some kind of terrible insect.
7. He thought of his family tenderly as he lay there, and, when the light began to come through the window, he died.

REVIEW, pages 110–111

Across	Down
1. brave	2. realize
3. managed to	4. Grab
7. soothed	5. disgusting
8. faint	6. cockroach
10. substance	9. terrified
12. beat	11. useless
13. smelly	

EXPAND

2, page 112

Answers will vary. The important task for the students is to become aware that while some synonyms have very similar meaning, others have elements both of similarity and dissimilarity.

3B GRAMMAR

2, page 114

2. f   3. g   4. a   5. c   6. b   7. e

3, page 114

2. His family locked Gregor in his room to keep him there.
3. His father grabbed a walking stick and newspaper to beat Gregor.
4. Grete went into Gregor's room every day to feed him.
5. Gregor followed Grete into the dining room to help her.
6. Gregor came out of his room to listen to the music.
7. His family took a train ride to celebrate his death.

REVISE

1, page 118

Answers will vary. Suggested answers:

2. small	5. ugly	8. fantastic
3. little	6. delicate	9. clear
4. curious	7. breathtaking	

UNIT 7

1C BACKGROUND AND VOCABULARY

2, page 123

1. g	3. a	5. i	7. b	9. j
2. d	4. h	6. e	8. c	10. f

READ FOR MAIN IDEAS, page 126

1. F: The Amish came to the United States and Canada to escape religious persecution.
2. F: children learn English at school.
3. T
4. F: Amish who choose to leave usually lose the opportunity to stay in touch with their family and friends.
5. F: Some Amish youth decide to join the outside world as a result of their experiences in *rumspringa*.
6. T

READ FOR DETAILS, pages 126–127

The following should be crossed out:

1. b   2. c   3. a   4. b   5. a   6. d

MAKE INFERENCES, page 127

1. S   3. L   5. S   7. S
2. L   4. S   6. L

2B READING TWO

2, page 130

Answers may vary. Suggested answers:

1. He didn't want to struggle with hard labor for very little financial reward.
2. He hoped to achieve financial security.
3. He was taught that the outside world is dangerous and evil.
4. He regrets that he lost contact with his Amish relatives.

STEP 1: Organize, page 130

Answers will vary. Suggested answers:

I. A. Isaac's father: struggled with hard labor and chores; raised a large family
   B. Isaac's mother: struggled with hard labor and chores; raised a large family
II. A. When Isaac left, he got a modern-style haircut.
    B. When Isaac left, he exchanged his Amish clothing for jeans.
III. A. Isaac left his parents a note to avoid their shock and tears.
     B. When Isaac left, his parents followed him to Ohio.
IV. A. Isaac regrets losing contact with his Amish relatives.
    B. Isaac only contacts his mother once or twice a year.
V. A. Isaac wanted to gain financial security.
   B. Now Isaac works full-time, attends college, and manages his properties.

REVIEW, page 132

The following words should be crossed out:

2. commitment   6. acceptance
3. improve   7. rewarding
4. equalize   8. stopped
5. change   9. wander
                10. shun

EXPAND

2, page 133

1. a   2. b   3. a   4. a   5. a   6. b

3B GRAMMAR

2, page 134

                           Wh-   S   V
Isaac and his brother discussed what they wanted to do.

                  Wh-   S   V
He understood why his parents were worried about him.

3, page 136

1. the people are wearing costumes
2. the Amish are
3. the Amish don't wear modern clothing or drive cars
4. the Amish believe in living separately from the rest of the world
5. the Amish believe in
6. the Amish don't use electricity
7. the Amish speak English

WRITE

1, pages 138–139

Answers may vary. Suggested answers:

1. moving to Rio
2. the beach; more money; better career
3. no place to live at first; high cost of living; leaving family and friends
4. possibility of a one-year contract with the hotel

2, page 139

II.
Supporting details: The hotel offered to pay more money. Working in a hotel was better for my career.

III.
Main idea: Moving to Rio had some disadvantages.
Supporting details: I had no place to live. Leaving my family and friends was difficult.

IV.
Conclusion: I'm happy with my choice.

REVISE

2, pages 140–141

1. Rio is well-known for lovely beaches and exciting nightlife.
2. The hotel will help me develop my career and earn more money.
3. If I go to Rio, I will have to leave my beloved family and my dear friends.
4. When I received the job offer, I couldn't believe my good luck and what the new job would pay.
5. My boss and my co-workers have a lot of experience in the hotel business.
6. When I told my mother I was leaving, she cried and told me she was proud of me.
7. At the hotel, I will develop my job skills and my career opportunities.
8. I will try to help hotel guests cheerfully and do my job efficiently.

UNIT 8

IC BACKGROUND AND VOCABULARY

1, pages 144–145

1. e	4. b, c	7. b, c	10. f
2. g	5. g	8. b	11. a
3. e	6. e	9. f	12. h

2, page 145

1. b	3. h	5. j	7. a	9. c
2. i	4. g	6. f	8. e	10. d

READ FOR MAIN IDEAS, page 147

1. d   2. b   3. e   4. a   5. c

READ FOR DETAILS, pages 147–148

Answers may vary. Suggested answers:

1. A matchmaker helped by finding someone of the right age and background.
2. A successful marriage was one that produced sons.
3. thirteen
4. They stopped night visits if they thought a boy might not be a good husband.
5. She would get pregnant.
6. She wouldn't be able to get married.
7. They believed unmarried women should not get pregnant.
8. It didn't continue to exist because John Noyes had left the community.
9. In 1890, polygamy was officially banned in the Mormon church.

MAKE INFERENCES, page 148

Answers will vary. Suggested answers:

a. 9   The boy and the girl were free to be together unless the girl's parents strongly objected to the boy.

b. 7–8   The boy and girl were free to be together, but the boy wouldn't marry a girl if she didn't become pregnant.

c. 1   The parents made the decision without asking the boy and girl.

d. 6–8   The boy and girl were free to marry whom they wanted, but if the husband later chose to take additional wives, the first wife couldn't prevent it.

e. 4–7   The boy and girl chose the Oneida Community, which was a free choice. Yet, by choosing this lifestyle, they agreed to accept any partner.

2B READING TWO

2, page 150

1. F   2. T   3. F   4. F   5. T

STEP 1: Organize, pages 150–151

Answers will vary. Suggested answers:

2. C; V	6. H; B	10. OC
3. C; V	7. C	11. M
4. B	8. H	12. H; B; M
5. H; M	9. B	

STEP 2: Synthesize, page 152

Traditional Hopi: A girl must become pregnant before she could marry to demonstrate her fertility. If the girl became pregnant, she could choose the boy she liked to marry. Marrying young was an important factor in choosing a spouse.

Old Bavarian: A girl must become pregnant before she could marry to demonstrate her fertility. If the girl became pregnant, the boy could ask her to marry him.

Oneida Community: Founded by John Noyes, men and women practiced group marriage, in which they changed partners frequently.

Early Mormon: Founded by Joseph Smith, this group practiced polygamy, a marriage in which a man could have more than one wife. Marrying young was an important factor in choosing a spouse.

REVIEW, page 153

b. C	d. W	f. M	h. W	j. C
c. M	e. C	g. C	i. M	k. M

EXPAND, pages 154–155

2. c; R	6. a; R	10. a; A
3. a; A	7. a; D	11. b; R
4. a; C / E	8. c; C / E	12. c; A
5. c; D	9. b; S	

3B GRAMMAR

2, page 156

1. a	3. a	5. a	7. a	9. the
2. the	4. a	6. a	8. a	10. The

3, page 157

1. a   2. a   3. b   4. a

REVISE

2, page 160

2. married	5. courtship	8. tradition
3. marriage	6. traditional	9. romantic
4. court	7. romance	10. similarity

UNIT 9

1C BACKGROUND AND VOCABULARY

2, page 166

1. a	3. a	5. b	7. b	9. a	11. a
2. a	4. a	6. a	8. b	10. b	

READ FOR MAIN IDEAS, page 169

2. F: The atmosphere is getting warmer.
3. F: We can't stop it, but if we act now, we can slow it and adapt.
4. T

READ FOR DETAILS, page 170

1. c, f, g, h	3. i	5. f, g, h	7. f	9. e
2. d	4. a	6. b	8. c	

MAKE INFERENCES, page 170

1. a   2. b   3. b   4. a

2B READING TWO

2, page 172

Answers will vary. Suggested answers:

1. International Panel on Climate Change
2. limits for gas emissions
3. to get attention and money for research
4. to support groups that discredit the idea of global warming
5. They think ExxonMobil tries to confuse with incorrect and dishonest information.

STEP 1: Organize, page 173

2a: Some gases get absorbed by plants to make food
2b: Some gases stay in atmosphere
3a: Some places get warmer
3b: Atmosphere gets more energetic (windier, wetter, drier)
4: Kyoto Protocol is signed.
5: Companies, such as ExxonMobil, hire scientists to discredit other scientists
6a: Public is confused
6b: Groups pressure ExxonMobil to stop being dishonest about climate change

REVIEW, pages 174–175

2. fossil fuels	6. sign	10. carbon dioxide
3. limited	7. evidence	11. adapt
4. link	8. atmosphere	12. reduce
5. escaped	9. energetic	13. climate

EXPAND, page 176

Answers will vary. Suggested answers:

2.	clear:	atmosphere, agreement, evidence, doubt, gas
3.	warm:	atmosphere, climate
4.	powerful:	fossil fuels, public, evidence
5.	energetic	atmosphere, government, production, climate
6.	harmful:	fossil fuels, gas, atmosphere, carbon dioxide, emissions, production, climate
7.	increasing:	gas, carbon dioxide, confusion, evidence, agreement, emissions, production, doubt
8.	national:	confusion, agreement, government
9.	obvious:	confusion, evidence, agreement, purpose, doubt
10.	massive:	confusion, evidence, emissions, production

3B GRAMMAR

2, pages 177–178

1. may / might / could	5. Will
2. may / might / could	6. Are . . . going to be
3. may / might / could	7. may / might / could
4. may / might / could	

REVISE

2, pages 181–182

2. As a result,	7. Therefore,
3. Consequently,	8. since
4. as	9. As a result,
5. As a result,	10. Because
6. Because	11. As

UNIT 10

1C BACKGROUND AND VOCABULARY

2, page 187

1. g	8. m
2. k	9. d
3. l	10. e
4. a	11. h
5. f	12. j
6. i	13. c
7. b	

READ FOR MAIN IDEAS, page 190

2. A	7. B
3. B	8. B
4. B	9. A
5. B	10. B
6. A	

READ FOR DETAILS, page 190

b. 10	g. 2
c. 6	h. 4
d. 8	i. 8
e. 9	j. 5
f. 1	

MAKE INFERENCES, page 191

1. "Without capital punishment, murderers are allowed to participate in and enjoy life."
2. "There are times when murder is not committed because of cruelty."
3. "Execution . . . sends a strong message to others who might kill: Killers will not be allowed to live."
4. "It also costs the taxpayer millions of dollars more to execute a criminal than to imprison that criminal for life."
5. "And let us not forget that murdering the murderer is a violent act in itself; it is revenge."

2B READING TWO, pages 192–194

Chart 1

1. 2007
2. 30 countries (*Answers to the second question will vary.*)
3. Against. More countries have abolished the death penalty or have not used it for decades.
4. *Answers will vary.*
5. *Answers will vary.*

Charts 2 and 3

6. It dropped because people were given another choice: life imprisonment without parole.
7. More people support life imprisonment than capital punishment.

Chart 4

8. *Suggested answer:* It shows that innocent people have been imprisoned or executed by mistake.
9. *Answers will vary.*

Chart 5

10. *Answers will vary. Suggested answer:* They exercise the death penalty. There are no European countries that have the death penalty.

STEP 1: Organize, page 195

2. F	7. O
3. F	8. F
4. F	9. O
5. F	10. O
6. O	

REVIEW, pages 197–198

2. cruel	6. innocent	10. rights
3. oppose	7. guilty	11. citizens
4. abolished	8. violent	12. support
5. Justice	9. respects	13. forgiveness

EXPAND

1, page 199

The abstract nouns are:

4. anger	9. citizenship	13. guilt
5. punishment	10. innocence	14. society
6. justice	12. government	15. rights

2, page 199

2. m	8. a
3. i	9. l
4. k	10. e
5. g	11. b
6. d	12. h
7. j	13. f

3, pages 200–201

2. criminal (weaker)	7. destroy (stronger)
3. cruel (stronger)	8. revenge (stronger)
4. loved ones (stronger)	9. end (weaker)
5. citizens (stronger)	10. passionate (weaker)
6. foreigners (neither)	11. recognize (weaker)

3B GRAMMAR

2, page 203

1. has been	6. has been coming
2. has been waiting	7. has always believed
3. has been writing	8. has been telling
4. has been	9. has loved
5. have visited	

3, page 203

1. Recently, 119 countries haven't used the death penalty.
2. 30 countries have not used the death penalty for 10 years.
3. China has been executing more than 1,000 people annually.

REVISE

2, pages 208–209

1. Wayne was the kind of guy that was never noticed at school, and he never got into trouble.
2. Since the police came to his house and arrested Wayne for murder, his life has never been the same.
3. Wayne was given the death penalty because he was found guilty at the end of his trial.
4. Wayne said that he was innocent, but the jury didn't believe him.
5. Wayne's life in jail is very different now although he still remembers his life before jail.
6. Wayne's mother doesn't want him to feel lonely, so she visits him almost every day.
7. When his lawyer visits him, Wayne asks about getting a new trial.

Unit Word List

The **Unit Word List** is a summary of key vocabulary from the student book. The words are presented by unit, in alphabetical order.

UNIT 1

campaign (noun)
catch the eye
catchy
commercial (noun and adjective)
competition
convince
exotic
fail
firm (noun)
global
goal
hold people's attention
impress
market (noun)
message
pay attention
succeed
successful

UNIT 2

astonishing
con man / woman
deception
duplicate (verb)
fake
fishy
fraud
honesty
impersonate
impress
motive
suspicious
weary

UNIT 3

achieve
athlete
awesome
benefit (noun and verb)
concentration
control (noun and verb)
controversy
energy
escape (noun and verb)
focus (noun and verb)
get hooked on
hooked on
intense
make it
mental
obsessed
obsession
perfect (verb)
perform
physical (adjective)
pressure (noun)
qualifying
style (noun)

UNIT 4

blunt (adjective)
compete
emphasize
fairly
feminine
gossip (verb)
identity
influence (verb)
juicy
lady-like
masculine
occupation
reflect
rough and tough
status
the dirt
women's movement

UNIT 5

beauty
coastal
consequences
continent (noun)
effect (noun)
environment
fragile
frozen
glaciers
harsh
huge
icebergs
inhabit
landscape (noun)
natural (adjective)
ozone layer
preserve (verb)
protection
remote (adjective)
research (noun and verb)
scenic
scientific
scientist
sunlight
temperature
tourist (noun)
vast

UNIT 6

awful
beat (verb)
beat up
brave (adjective)
certainly
cockroach
comprehend
cry (verb)
disgusting
enter
faint (verb)
grab (verb)
knock (noun)
manage to
pierce
realize
smelly
soothe
stinky
substance
surely
tap (noun)
terrible
terrified
useless
weep

UNIT 7

allowed
be up in the air
bond (noun)
conveniences
decline (verb)
establish
maintain
open up a can of worms
persecution
pious
settle down
socialize
stuck between a rock
   and a hard place
the deciding factor
the pros and cons
turn (someone) down

UNIT 8

arranged marriage
background
bride
broken heart
characteristics
commitment
courtship
enduring
engagement
everlasting
faith
faithfully
fertility
groom (noun)
infertility
lasting
leadership
polygamy
pregnancy
pregnant
produce (verb)
proud
raise (verb)
religion
romance
romantic
spouse
support (verb)
traditional

UNIT 9

adapt
agreement
atmosphere
carbon dioxide
climate
coal
confusion
doubt (noun)
emissions
energetic
escape (verb)
evidence
fossil fuels
gases
government
harmful
limited
link (noun)
massive
obvious
production
public (adjective)
purpose
reduce
sign (noun)

UNIT 10

abolish
abolition
anger
citizen
citizenship
crime
cruel
cruelty
destroy
execution
fairness
foreigner
forgiveness
guilt
guilty
immigrant
immigration
innocence
innocent
justice
loved ones
murderer
oppose
opposition
passionate
punishment
respect (verb)
revenge (noun)
right (noun)
society
support (verb)
violent

Achievement Tests
Unit 1

PART I: READING

1.1 *Read the passage about global marketing. Check (✔) the best prediction of how Frito-Lay will adapt* Cheetos *for sale in China. There is only one right answer.*

The snack food *Cheetos,* as the name suggests, is made with cheese. Frito-Lay stated its goal to introduce *Cheetos* to the Chinese market. However, the company had an immediate problem: How do you convince Chinese consumers to buy *Cheetos* when they generally don't like cheese? Frito-Lay responded to the problem. It showed that the company could adapt its products and advertising to the global market.

_____ **A.** by changing their color   _____ **C.** by changing their shape

_____ **B.** by making them without cheese   _____ **D.** by making them sweeter

1.2 *Now read the entire article. Use the information to choose the correct answers.*

Cheetos in China

The snack food *Cheetos,* as the name suggests, is made with cheese. Frito-Lay stated its goal to introduce *Cheetos* to the Chinese market. However, the company had an immediate problem: How do you convince Chinese consumers to buy *Cheetos* when they generally don't like cheese? Frito-Lay responded to the problem. It showed that the company could adapt its products and advertising to the global market.

Cheetos, in China, are cheeseless. The company experimented with exotic flavors such as Peking duck, fried egg, and even dog. Finally, it chose two winners: butter flavor (called "American Cream") and barbequed beef ("Japanese Steak"). A third flavor, "Crispy Fresh Seafood," followed after that. The three flavors are very successful.

Frito-Lay knew it needed new flavors and new marketing to catch the eye of Chinese consumers. The company began to operate under the name *Leshi,* which means "happy things," in China. The company also changed the product packaging. In America, bags of *Cheetos* have pictures of *Chester the Cheetah,* a cartoon cat. In China, Chester was replaced with a picture of a red sun.

After *Cheetos,* Frito-Lay successfully introduced its potato chips to China. When the chips failed to sell at first, Frito-Lay created TV commercials for the chips. These commercials showed potatoes being cut. This was to show people where the chips came from. The company created advertising messages to impress girls and young women. "We market to girls and the boys follow," says China sales director Jackson Chiu. Chiu was able to raise sales by 57 percent in one year.

Frito-Lay has had to make quick changes at times. Once, China stopped potato imports from other countries. Frito-Lay quickly bought two farms in China to grow their own potatoes. Now other companies are paying attention to Frito-Lay's success in China.

"They are doing an impressive job," says Nevada University business professor Tom Hastings.

Check (✔) the best answer to complete each sentence.

1. A popular flavor of *Cheetos* in China is _____.

   _____ **A.** Peking duck

   _____ **B.** fresh seafood

   _____ **C.** fried egg

   _____ **D.** sweet and sour

2. To sell its potato chips in China, Frito-Lay created new _____.

   _____ **A.** flavors

   _____ **B.** bag sizes

   _____ **C.** advertising

   _____ **D.** cartoon cats

3. Frito-Lay sells an "American Cream" flavor in China because

   _____.

   _____ **A.** China prohibited cheese imports

   _____ **B.** it is the most popular flavor in the world

   _____ **C.** young girls and women liked the name

   _____ **D.** Chinese consumers preferred that flavor

4. In China, bags of *Cheetos* have a picture of _____.

   _____ **A.** happy things

   _____ **B.** a cartoon cat

   _____ **C.** a Japanese steak

   _____ **D.** a red sun

5. At first, Chinese consumers didn't buy Frito-Lay potato chips because they

   _____.

   _____ **A.** didn't like the flavor

   _____ **B.** knew they were from an American company

   _____ **C.** were not sure where the chips came from

   _____ **D.** preferred potato chips made in China

1.3 *Read the passage from "Changing World Markets" in* NorthStar: Reading and Writing *3, Unit 1. Use the information from this reading and "Cheetos in China" to complete the activity. Not all of the details will be used. The first one has been done for you.*

Changing World Markets

Good morning. It's good to be here with you all. My goal today is to give you some information about changing world markets. Let's start by looking at the U.S.A. Can you think of a country with more advertising than the United States? Think about watching a movie on TV. You're waiting for the good guy to get the bad guy, and suddenly there's a commercial. A few minutes later, the good guy is in trouble, and you're interrupted by another commercial. Message after message. It's not like that in other countries. In places like France and Spain, you can watch at least a half hour of the program before a commercial interruption. And then the commercials come all at once.

China is a different story. For years, any kind of commercial advertising was illegal. Government advertising was seen everywhere, but business advertising was nonexistent. Then Sony came along and changed things. The Japanese company led the way for others to come into the country. We can learn something from Sony, too. It's important not to come and start advertising too quickly because that can lead to serious mistakes. Advertisers must take their time and plan their campaigns carefully. They should also consider the type of advertising that is most popular. In China, large public billboards[1] are the cheapest and most common way to advertise. They were used in the past for official government messages and are still used today.

When you're dealing with international markets, you're dealing with different customs, different tastes. Consider Coca-Cola in Brazil. The company sells a drink flavored with *guarana,* an exotic[2] South American fruit. They've been successful in selling it during the February holiday with this message: "the flavor of Carnaval."

As you know, things are changing every day. New markets are opening up all the time. We have to consider laws and customs before we start planning a campaign. We also need to think about our product. Will people be able to buy it? Regarding our marketing plan, will people understand it? Remember that for years in China and Russia, people had a hard time buying things. The best advertisement of all was a long line in front of a store. That's how people knew which store was the place to go. So we must think about how things are changing if we expect to be successful. I appreciate your attendance today. It's been a pleasure to be with you.

---

[1] **billboards:** large signs used for advertising, usually outdoors
[2] **exotic:** unusual and exciting because of a connection with a foreign country

> **Details**
>
> - Tom Hastings admires Frito-Lay.
> - Advertising used to be illegal in China.
> - ~~Brazilians like the guarana fruit.~~
> - Frito-Lay changed the picture on the *Cheetos* bag from a cartoon cat to a red sun.
> - Most Chinese consumers don't like cheese.
> - Billboard advertising is common in China.
> - Advertisements interrupt TV movies.
> - China prohibited the import of potatoes.

Main Idea	Details	
	"Changing World Markets"	**"*Cheetos* in China"**
International markets have different tastes.	Brazilians like the guarana fruit.	3.
Companies must consider which types of advertising are most popular.	1.	4.
Companies must consider laws when planning a campaign.	2.	5.

PART 2: VOCABULARY

2.1 *Cross out the vocabulary item in each group that does not relate to the others.*

1. advertisement   impression   message   commercial

2. impress   succeed   catch the eye   hold people's attention

3. competition   global   international   worldwide

2.2 *Read the story. Use the words from the box to fill in the blanks. Not all of the words will be used.*

campaign	caught the eye	competition	exotic	message
catchy	commercials	convinced	global	paid attention

American ice cream maker *Ben & Jerry's* recently introduced its product to England.

The company has been successful thanks to clever marketing. First, *Ben & Jerry's*

created a unique advertising _____. The company paid to put
                              1.

advertising on the sides of cows, something which _____ of
                                                    2.

passing drivers. When the story appeared in British newspapers, many people

_____, and suddenly *Ben & Jerry's* was a well-known product. The
       3.

company also created TV _____. They feature _____
                           4.   **5.**

music and the _____ "If it's not fun, why do it?"
                 6.

PART 3: SKILLS FOR WRITING

3.1 *Read the sentences. Write the verbs in parentheses in the correct tense (simple present or present progressive).*

1. These days, Frito-Lay _____ with new flavors.
                          (experiment)

2. Every year, the company _____ a new flavor.
                             (introduce)

3. This year, Frito-Lay _____ a "French chicken wings" flavor.
                          (introduce)

4. Frito-Lay often _____ on billboards in China.
                     (advertise)

5. At the moment, sales of *Cheetos* _____ quickly.
                                        (increase)

6. Most Americans _____ seafood is a strange flavor for chips.
                    (think)

3.2　*Read the paragraph. Four sentences do not support the underlined topic sentence. Write those four sentences on the lines.*

<u>Domino's Pizza has become a successful global business by changing the flavor of its pizzas to meet local preferences.</u> For example, Domino's has a mayonnaise and potato pizza in Tokyo. They also sell a seafood pizza there. In India, Domino's customers can order a pickled ginger pizza. Frito-Lay is also successful in India. Domino's restaurants in Singapore sell a spicy chili pizza. I do not like spicy food very much, so I wouldn't order it! One of the strangest flavors is reindeer sausage pizza, which is very popular in Iceland. Even in England, which has many similar foods to the U.S., Domino's pizza is different. English customers can order boiled egg and corn on their pizzas. Some British people put corn in sandwiches. In France, people put corn in salads. These flavors may sound strange to Americans, but they are an important part of Domino's global business.

1. _____

2. _____

3. _____

4. _____

PART 4: WRITING

A Paragraph (20 minutes)

Write about a foreign product that people can buy in your country.

- Describe the product.
- Say whether the product is successful or not and explain why.
- Write a clear topic sentence.
- Write detail sentences that clearly support your topic sentence.
- Use the vocabulary and grammar from Unit 1.

Unit I Vocabulary Words				
catch the eye	competition	fail to sell	hold people's attention	message
catchy	convince	global	impress	pay attention
commercial	exotic	goal	market	successful

Unit I Grammar: Simple Present and Present Progressive	
[simple present] • People in Spain rarely ***order*** pizzas.	[present progressive] • The world ***is changing*** quickly.

Achievement Tests
Unit 2

Name: _____

Date: _____

PART 1: READING

1.1 *Read the passage about Internet bank fraud. Check (✔) the best prediction of what the reading is about. There is only one right answer.*

According to the U.S. government, Americans lose an astonishing $200 million a year to Internet bank fraud. It is often difficult for police to identify and arrest the criminals behind these crimes. One woman, however, decided to take action herself.

_____ **A.** joining the police

_____ **B.** fighting criminals

_____ **C.** reporting bank fraud

_____ **D.** protecting our identities

1.2 *Now read the entire article. Use the information to choose the correct answers.*

Bank Fraud by E-mail

According to the U.S. government, Americans lose an astonishing $200 million a year to Internet bank fraud. It is often difficult for police to identify and arrest the criminals behind these crimes. One woman, however, decided to take action herself. Weary of receiving fishy e-mail offers, Julia Hargood, a college professor in Houston, Texas, decided to teach one con man a lesson.

Julia received an e-mail from a man saying he was a rich politician who needed her help. She immediately knew it was suspicious. In the e-mail, the man said he needed to hide some money and wanted to put $8 million in Julia's bank account. He asked for her bank information. The man told Julia she could keep $2 million for helping him. Instead of deleting the e-mail like she normally did, she decided to reply.

In her reply, Julia lied and told the man she was the leader of a group of religious singers. She called the fake organization "The Sacred Sisters of Sound." Julia promised to help the man if he joined her group. To join the group, Julia told him he had to sing a special song. She sent him another e-mail with instructions on how to sing the song. The con man was impressed by her story and sent a recording of himself singing (the "special song" was actually from a children's TV show). In the next e-mail, Julia asked the con man to send $60 for an "application fee." Again, the con man believed her and sent the money. At that point, Julia told the con man she had deceived him. She gave the $60 to charity.

"My motive was to show him how much it hurts to be deceived—not just financially, but emotionally as well," Julia says. Julia doesn't recommend that other people try to duplicate her success. "The best thing to do is delete suspicious e-mails or contact the police."

Check (✔) the best answer to complete each sentence.

1. Julia decided to reply to the con man's message because she wanted

   _____.

   _____ **A.** him to give her money

   _____ **B.** him to join her organization

   _____ **C.** to hear him sing

   _____ **D.** to teach him a lesson

2. The con man thought Julia was being _____.

   _____ **A.** honest

   _____ **B.** strange

   _____ **C.** weary

   _____ **D.** suspicious

3. Julia probably asked the man to sing in order to _____.

   _____ **A.** impersonate him

   _____ **B.** identify him

   _____ **C.** embarrass him

   _____ **D.** motivate him

4. The con man sent Julia _____.

   _____ **A.** $8 million

   _____ **B.** $2 million

   _____ **C.** $200

   _____ **D.** $60

5. The best title for this story is _____.

   _____ **A.** "The Importance of Honesty"

   _____ **B.** "The Sacred Sisters of Sound"

   _____ **C.** "The High Cost of Bank Fraud"

   _____ **D.** "How to Con a Con Man"

1.3 *Read the passage from "The Michelle Brown Story: Identity Theft" in* NorthStar: Reading and Writing 3, *Unit 2. Use the information from this reading and "Bank Fraud by E-mail" to complete the activity. Not all of the details will be used. The first one has been done for you.*

The Michelle Brown Story: Identity Theft

Someone else was using her name, her address, her social security number, and her driver's license. It was as if someone was slowly erasing her identity . . .

When her credit report arrived, there were delinquent[1] bills on it for thousands of dollars, including a sizable phone bill and even a bill for liposuction treatments.[2] What was this? She became afraid to open her own mailbox, for fear of what new debt would be awaiting her. In time, she would learn that there was an arrest warrant[3] out for Michelle Brown in Texas. The charge was conspiracy[4] to sell marijuana. She had never broken a law, any law. How could she be wanted by the police?

She began to worry that the other Michelle Brown would break into her apartment in search of her passport or checks, or who knew what else. Whenever she got home after dark she carried a flashlight and searched through the rooms, including every closet. She was weary and angry. When she went to bed at night, she was scared. If she heard the slightest noise, her first thought was that the woman calling herself Michelle Brown was out there in the dark, right beneath her window. Who was this person who was stealing her identity? Why of all the people in the world, did she pick her? And what did she want?

---

[1] **delinquent:** late in paying money that is owed
[2] **liposuction treatments:** a type of cosmetic surgery in which body fat is removed
[3] **arrest warrant:** a document giving police the authority to take someone to jail
[4] **conspiracy:** a secret plan by two or more people to do something illegal

---

Details

- Another woman was calling herself Michelle Brown.
- Americans lose $200 million a year to fraud.
- Julia was weary of fishy e-mail offers.
- She felt scared and angry.

- There was an arrest warrant for drugs.
- A man said he was a rich politician.
- The man offered Julia $2 million.
- ~~Michelle had bills for thousands of dollars.~~

Main Idea	Details	
	"The Michelle Brown Story: Identity Theft"	**"Bank Fraud by E-mail"**
Con men hurt people financially.	Michelle had bills for thousands of dollars.	3.
Con men hurt people emotionally.	1.	4.
Con men often impersonate other people.	2.	5.

PART 2: VOCABULARY

2.1 *Complete the chart with the correct word forms.*

Noun	Verb	Adjective	Adverb
1.	2.	suspicious	3.
deception	4.	5.	6.
7.	impersonate	X	X

2.2 *Read the story. Use the words from the box to fill in the blanks. Not all of the words will be used.*

deception	honesty	impressing	suspicious
fishy	impersonating	motive	weary

I had a scary phone conversation with a con man last week. The man was

_____ a government agent. He asked me for my name, address,
1.

passport number, and social security number. I knew something was

_____, so I didn't tell him anything. I hung up and called the police
2.

instead. They said I was right to be _____. The police said the man's
3.

_____ was to steal my identity.
4.

PART 3: SKILLS FOR WRITING

3.1 *Read the story. Write the verbs in parentheses in the correct tense (simple past or past progressive).*

I had a frustrating experience with bank fraud. I ___was living___ in
(live)

Los Angeles when another person _____ my bank information. I
1. (steal)

_____ this while I _____ through my bank
2. (discover)   3. (look)

statements. I immediately _____ my bank. I thought of so many
4. (call)

questions while I _____ to the bank agent. Why would somebody do
5. (talk)

that to me? And how?

3.2 *Read the paragraphs. Check (✔) the best topic sentence.*

1. _____. The lawyer promised to
help her get U.S. citizenship. She paid him more than a thousand dollars. At first, he
said he was working hard to help her, but then suddenly, he disappeared. She never
heard from him again, and she lost the money.

_____ **A.** My sister wanted to become a U.S. citizen.

_____ **B.** My sister was so angry and hurt.

_____ **C.** My sister had a terrible experience with a fake lawyer.

_____ **D.** My sister says you can't trust everyone you meet.

2. _____. He offered me three
boxes of computer equipment for a really low price. I thought it was a good deal.
He opened the first box and showed me the equipment inside, and I agreed to buy
all three. When I got home and opened the other two boxes, they were filled with
sand. The computer equipment in the first box was broken. I called the police, but
they never found the man.

_____ **A.** I had a bad experience with boxes of sand.

_____ **B.** A dishonest man cheated me out of some money.

_____ **C.** I am angry because I bought some broken computer equipment.

_____ **D.** I met a man in a parking lot near the university library.

3. _____. Someone opened five credit cards in my name and spent close to twenty thousand dollars. My credit was destroyed. At first, the police couldn't help me. I couldn't sleep at night, and I was so stressed I started eating less. I couldn't focus at work and almost lost my job. It took me three years to fix my credit and get my life back together, and I still have nightmares.

    _____ **A.** I lost a lot of money because of identity theft.

    _____ **B.** It was the worst day of my life.

    _____ **C.** I had a frustrating experience with a con man.

    _____ **D.** Identity theft nearly destroyed my life.

PART 4: WRITING

A Story (20 minutes)

Reread "Bank Fraud by E-mail." Then write a paragraph telling the same story from the con man's point of view.

- Pretend you are the con man in the story. Use first person ("I").
- Describe what happened. Use details from Julia's story.
- Write a clear topic sentence to focus your paragraph.
- Write detail sentences that support the topic sentence.
- Write a concluding sentence to say what happened at the end.
- Use the vocabulary and grammar from Unit 2.

Unit 2 Vocabulary Words					
astonishing	duplicate	fishy	honesty	impress	suspicious
deception	fake	fraud	impersonate	motive	weary
Unit 2 Grammar: Simple Past and Past Progressive					
[simple past] [past progressive] • I **replied** to her first e-mail while I **was drinking** my morning cup of tea.					

Achievement Tests
Unit 3

Name: _____

Date: _____

PART 1: READING

1.1 *Read the passage about an extreme sport. Check (✔) the best prediction of what the reading is about. There is only one right answer.*

Jeffrey Tillman, age nine, has a new favorite sport: World's Strongest Man. "It's totally awesome. They carry cars and stuff," he explains. In World's Strongest Man, athletes from around the world demonstrate their physical perfection in five extreme events. All of the events require super-human strength. These days the sport is quickly winning fans around the world. Some people, however, are starting to worry that the sport has a dark side.

_____ **A.** the strategy of the sport _____ **C.** the pros and cons of the sport

_____ **B.** the benefit of the sport _____ **D.** the origin of the sport

1.2 *Now read the entire article. Use the information to choose the correct answers.*

Going to Extremes

Jeffrey Tillman, age nine, has a new favorite sport: World's Strongest Man. "It's totally awesome. They carry cars and stuff," he explains. Jeffrey's room is decorated with pictures of Phil Pfister and Mariusz Pudzianowski. These are winners of the 2006 and 2007 World's Strongest Man championships. In World's Strongest Man, athletes from around the world demonstrate their physical perfection in five extreme events. All of the events require super-human strength. The events change every year, but past events have included carrying huge rocks, repeatedly lifting tree trunks,[1] and even running with a refrigerator under each arm. One of the most intense events involves pulling an airplane from one end of a road to another. "It's a great competition," says Tomas Kaminski, a Polish fan of the sport. "To win, you have to be strong, fast, and have great concentration." These days, the sport is quickly winning fans around the world. Some people, however, are starting to worry that the sport has a dark side.

The case of American competitor Jesse Marunde showed the danger of going to extremes. Marunde achieved second place in the 2005 World's Strongest Man championship. Two years later he died of a heart attack. Now, some doctors suspect Marunde's death was because of steroid[2] use. They worry the same thing will happen to other competitors. "There is so much pressure to become stronger," says Dr. Amir Bachchan, a professor of health policy at New York University. "They become obsessed with winning, and this leads to injury and sometimes steroid abuse." Bachchan hopes other competitors learn from Marunde's case. "They need to understand there is more to lose than there is to win."

---

[1] **tree trunk:** the body of a tree, with no leaves and branches
[2] **steroids:** illegal drugs that increase muscle strength but cause health problems

Check (✔) the best answer to complete each sentence.

1. To win World's Strongest Man, competitors need strength, speed, and

   _____.

   _____ **A.** patience

   _____ **B.** focus

   _____ **C.** a unique style

   _____ **D.** a good coach

2. One World's Strongest Man event involves _____.

   _____ **A.** running with tree trunks

   _____ **B.** carrying huge rocks

   _____ **C.** lifting airplanes

   _____ **D.** throwing refrigerators

3. Jesse Marunde died in _____.

   _____ **A.** 2004

   _____ **B.** 2005

   _____ **C.** 2006

   _____ **D.** 2007

4. World's Strongest Man sport is best described as _____.

   _____ **A.** popular with fans, but dangerous for competitors

   _____ **B.** dangerous for competitors, but popular with doctors

   _____ **C.** popular with doctors, but dangerous for fans

   _____ **D.** dangerous for fans, but popular with competitors

5. When Bachchan says, "there is more to lose than there is to win," he means

   _____.

   _____ **A.** the prize money for winners is not enough

   _____ **B.** most people will not win the championship

   _____ **C.** good health is more important than winning

   _____ **D.** every competitor should try to reach perfection

1.3 *Read the passage from "High School Star Hospitalized for Eating Disorder" in*
NorthStar: Reading and Writing 3, Unit 3. Use the information from this reading and
"Going to Extremes" to complete the activity. The first one has been done for you.

High School Star Hospitalized for Eating Disorder

Sierra High School gymnast Ashley Lindermann was hospitalized Tuesday for complications related to anorexia nervosa. Her coach, Dianne Coyle, says that she will not be returning to the gymnastics team this season.

"It's really a loss—not only to the team but also to Ashley personally," says Coyle. "She had hopes of qualifying for the Olympics. But her health comes first, of course. Once she is better, I'm sure she can get back into the sport and go for the gold."

Dr. Paula Kim, director of the Eating Disorders Clinic at Baldwin Hospital, explains that it is not unusual for athletes, especially gymnasts, to become obsessed with their weight. One reason for this is that in gymnastics, the lighter the body, the more skillfully it can perform. She explains that an obsession with weight can lead to extreme dieting, which affects not only the body but also the mind.

High school counselor Lisa Rodriguez has expressed concern that Lindermann's illness is related to pressure.

"There's an enormous amount of pressure that goes along with training for the Olympics," she says.

Since joining the Sierra High gymnastics team as a sophomore two years ago, Ashley has broken all school records and led the team to three regional championships.

Coach Coyle says, "All I can say is that I'm very, very sorry that Ashley got sick."

Coyle's concern for Lindermann's health is shared by her teammates and friends. Some of them recall how the tiny gymnastics star worked out at the health club in addition to hours of regular practice with the team.

Lindermann, who currently weighs only 72 pounds (32.6 kgs.), is expected to remain in the hospital for at least a few months.

Statement	Ashley Lindermann	Jesse Marunde	Both
She / he was an athlete.			✓
1. She / he felt a lot of pressure.			
2. She / he wanted bigger muscles.			
3. She / he wanted a lighter body.			
4. She / he achieved success.			

PART 2: VOCABULARY

2.1 *Read the paragraph. Use the words from the box to fill in the blanks. Not all of the words will be used.*

achieve	control	escape	intense	style
benefits	controversy	hooked on	pressure	

Why do some high school students become obsessed with sports? Experts say

one reason is sports let students _____ from the problems

1.

they experience at home or at school. These problems often include

_____ to get into a top university, or family situations that the

2.

students cannot _____. One expert says, "Obviously, sports have

3.

many _____, such as exercise and teamwork. The problem is when

4.

students become _____ sports, they can forget what is really

5.

important in life."

2.2 *Complete the chart with the correct word forms.*

Noun	Verb	Adjective	Adverb
perfection	perfect	perfect	perfectly
I.	achieve	achieved	X
athlete	X	athletic	2.
obsession	3.	4.	obsessively
benefit	benefit	5.	6.

PART 3: SKILLS FOR WRITING

3.1 *Read the sentences. Check (✔) the two modals that make each sentence correct.*

Dr. Paula Kim _____ say that many athletes become obsessed with their weight. She knows this from her work.

___✓___ can   _____ could   ___✓___ is able to

_____ can't   _____ couldn't   _____ wasn't able to

1. Phil Pfister is very strong. Now he _____ lift a tree trunk. In fact, he does this every week to practice.

   _____ can   _____ could   _____ is able to

   _____ can't   _____ couldn't   _____ wasn't able to

2. There was a gymnastics competition last night. Ashley Lindermann was in the hospital. She _____ go to the competition.

   _____ can   _____ could   _____ is able to

   _____ can't   _____ couldn't   _____ wasn't able to

3.2 *Read the paragraph. The reader needs more information about five words in addition to the underlined word. Write the words on the lines.*

Steroids are drugs that can increase muscle strength but cause health problems. Steroids are illegal according to the <u>CSA</u>. According to ONDCP, there are two ways of taking steroids. The first way is "stacking." The second way is called "pyramiding." Frederickson says steroids are common in high schools. Forty percent of high school students said steroids were "easy to obtain," according to a study.

1. _____

2. _____

3. _____

4. _____

5. _____

PART 4: WRITING

A Factual Report (20 minutes)

Write a one-paragraph report about the strongest person you know.

- State the main idea of the paragraph in your topic sentence.
- In the supporting details, answer the questions *who, what, when, where,* and *why* or *how* about this person.
- Give facts, examples, and explanations to support the details.
- Restate the main idea in your concluding sentence.
- Use the vocabulary and grammar from Unit 3.

Unit 3 Vocabulary Words					
achieve	benefit	controversy	focus	obsessed	pressure
athlete	concentration	escape	hooked on	perfect	style
awesome	control	extreme	intense	physical	

Unit 3 Grammar: Ability: *Can, Could, Be able to*
• Jeff ***can*** carry me on his shoulders. • She ***was able to*** run twenty miles.

Achievement Tests
Unit 4

Name: _____

Date: _____

PART 1: READING

1.1 *Read the passage about gender difference. Check (✔) the best prediction of what the reading is about. There is only one right answer.*

Who talks more, men or women? In North America, most people assume the answer is women. They think of long conversations between female friends and women's supposed love of juicy gossip. In truth, the answer to the question of who talks more depends on location. Studies by linguist Deborah Tannen show that women talk more at home. However, men talk more in public places, such as parties, meetings, and classrooms. Tannen believes the difference is due to gender identity.

_____ **A.** communication   _____ **C.** friendship

_____ **B.** marriage   _____ **D.** education

1.2 *Now read the entire article. Use the information to choose the correct answers.*

Gender and Conversation

Who talks more, men or women? In North America, most people assume the answer is women. They think of long conversations between female friends and women's supposed love of juicy gossip. In truth, the answer to the question of who talks more depends on location. Studies by linguist Deborah Tannen show that women talk more at home. However, men talk more in public places, such as parties, meetings, and classrooms. Tannen believes the difference is due to gender identity.

According to Tannen, it is masculine to give orders and show how much knowledge one possesses. In contrast, it is feminine to give suggestions and speak politely. Tannen says this explains why men like to talk a lot during business meetings and classroom discussions. They also like to talk during a dinner party with a larger group of people. Men can achieve higher status within the group if they talk a lot, direct conversation, display lots of knowledge, and influence others. In these situations, women may want to say more, but often do not. It does not seem lady-like to interrupt and compete with men for attention. Men, in contrast, are more willing to interrupt. They may not mind when other men interrupt them.

These differences may explain the discoveries of social researcher Patricia Dinkelaker. In a study of professional men and women, Dinkelaker found that women prefer "familial" work environments. This is where decisions are made in groups. But men prefer "hierarchical" organizations.[1] In such organizations, there is always a clear leader. Essentially, men and women want to work in an environment that fits their communication style.

In sum, gender identity affects not only *how* people speak, but *where* and *when*. It even affects the careers we choose.

_____

[1] **hierarchical organization:** the military, for example

Check (✔) the best answer to complete each sentence.

1. Tannen thinks men tend to be quieter at _____.

    _____ **A.** work

    _____ **B.** school

    _____ **C.** home

    _____ **D.** parties

2. Tannen says men talk in order to _____.

    _____ **A.** create strong friendships

    _____ **B.** achieve status in groups

    _____ **C.** escape stress from work

    _____ **D.** show their agreement

3. Tannen says women tend to speak less in public because _____.

    _____ **A.** men interrupt women when they talk

    _____ **B.** they choose the wrong occupations

    _____ **C.** people will gossip if women talk too much

    _____ **D.** public talk isn't considered feminine

4. Overall, men's conversations are best described as _____.

    _____ **A.** fair

    _____ **B.** competitive

    _____ **C.** impolite

    _____ **D.** short

5. These communication differences may affect how women choose

    _____.

    _____ **A.** husbands

    _____ **B.** jobs

    _____ **C.** friends

    _____ **D.** schools

1.3 *Read this passage from "Different Ways of Talking" in* NorthStar: Reading and Writing *3, Unit 4. Use the information from this reading and "Gender and Conversation" to complete the activity. Not all of the details will be used. The first one has been done for you.*

Different Ways of Talking

Different ways of speaking are part of gender. As adults, men and women sometimes face difficulties in their communication with each other. Studies of communication show that if a woman tells her husband about a problem, she will expect him to listen and offer sympathy. She may be annoyed when he simply tells her how to solve the problem. Similarly, a husband may be annoyed when his wife wants to stop and ask a stranger for directions to a park or restaurant. Unlike his wife, he would rather use a map and find his way by himself.

Language is also part of the different ways that men and women think about friendship. Most North American men believe that friendship means doing things together such as camping or playing tennis. Talking is not an important part of friendship for most of them. American women, on the other hand, usually identify their best friend as someone with whom they talk frequently. Tannen believes that for women, talking with friends and agreeing with them is very important. Tannen has found that women, in contrast to men, often use tag questions. For example, a woman might say, "This is a great restaurant, isn't it?" By adding a tag question to her speech ("isn't it?"), she is giving other people a chance to agree with her. Likewise, many women use more polite forms—"Can you close the door?" "Could you help me?" "Would you come here?" Men, however, often speak more directly, giving direct commands—"Close the door." "Help me." "Come here."

These differences seem to be part of growing up in the culture of the United States and following its rules of gender. If men and women can understand that many of their differences are cultural, not personal, they may be able to improve their relationships. They may begin to understand that because of gender differences in language, there is more than one way to communicate.

> **Details**
> - They use fewer commands.
> - Husbands and wives annoy each other.
> - Men enjoy camping or playing tennis.
> - Men want to achieve status.
> - They don't interrupt as often.
> - ~~Women want to develop friendships.~~
> - Women prefer "familial" organizations.
> - Women want to say more, but don't.

Main Idea	Details	
	"Different Ways of Talking"	**"Gender and Conversation"**
Men and women have different purposes for conversation.	Women want to develop friendships.	3.
In many ways, women speak more politely than men.	1.	4.
Communication differences can cause problems.	2.	5.

PART 2: VOCABULARY

2.1 *Read the story. Use the words from the box to fill in the blanks. Not all of the words will be used.*

beauty	consequence	feminine	juicy	status
bluntly	emphasized	gender	reflect	the dirt
compete	fairly	influences	rough and tough	

When Sarah Jordan came home from work, the first thing she wanted to do was tell her husband the latest gossip from her office. She was excited because she had just found out _____ on a coworker she didn't like. When she started to
1.

tell her husband the _____ details, he _____ said,
2.   **3.**

"Who cares? That's not my problem." Sarah felt hurt and annoyed at her husband.

Deborah Tannen says this is a typical example of _____
4.

difference. Sarah wants her husband to be a friend, and for Sarah, friendship is based on conversation. The way Sarah grew up _____ her opinion.
5.

Sarah's idea of what is _____ comes from her female friends and
6.

relatives. They have all _____ the importance of conversation in
7.

friendship to her.

Sarah's husband, on the other hand, has a different idea, also because of his childhood experience. As a child, his friends showed him the importance of being

_____. They taught him that talk was not about making friends,
8.

but achieving _____. With Sarah, he feels no need to
9.

_____, and therefore, no need to talk, unlike when he is at work.
10.

PART 3: SKILLS FOR WRITING

3.1   *Read the sentences. Fill in the blanks with the correct comparative form of the adverb in parentheses.*

Men are not always polite when they speak. Women are usually more polite.

Generally, women speak ___more politely than___ men.
                        (politely)

1. Male friends often talk only once a week. Female friends may talk every day.

    Usually, female friends talk _____ male friends.
                                    (frequently)

2. Boys' games always need a winner. Girls often don't care who wins.

    In general, girls play _____ boys.
                             (competitively)

3. Men are sometimes very direct in conversation. Women prefer to be more

    indirect. Often, women don't speak _____ men.
                                          (directly)

4. Men sometimes interrupt at meetings. Usually, women don't do this.

    People say men don't listen _____ women.
                                  (patiently)

3.2   *Read the sentences. Check (✔) the transitions that make the sentence correct. There are three transitions in number 1 and two transitions in number 2.*

Boys tend to play in large groups _____ girls, who usually play in smaller groups.

_____ however   ✔ in contrast to

_____ on the other hand   _____ in contrast

✔ unlike

1. Men rarely use tag questions in English. Women, _____, often use them.

    _____ however   _____ in contrast to

    _____ on the other hand   _____ in contrast

    _____ unlike

2. Men, _____ women, like to point out the other side of arguments.

    _____ however   _____ in contrast to

    _____ on the other hand   _____ in contrast

    _____ unlike

PART 4: WRITING

A Contrast Paragraph (20 minutes)

Write a paragraph in which you contrast the communication styles of one man and one woman you know.

- State the main idea of the paragraph in your topic sentence.
- Tell the reader which man and woman you will talk about.
- Give clear examples and details that show how their communication styles are different.
- Use transitions of contrast: *unlike, on the other hand, however,* etc.
- Use the vocabulary and grammar from Unit 4.

Unit 4 Vocabulary Words					
blunt	fairly	gossip	juicy	occupation	status
compete	feminine	identity	lady-like	reflect	the dirt
emphasize	gender	influence	masculine	rough and tough	women's movement

Unit 4 Grammar: Comparative Adverbs
[comparative adverb] • My father listens **more quietly than** my mother.

Achievement Tests
Unit 5

Name: _____

Date: _____

PART 1: READING

1.1 *Read the passage about eco-tourism. Check (✔) the best prediction of what the reading is about. There is only one right answer.*

Around the world, millions of people are worried about the harsh consequences of global warming. For now, however, there is at least one place that is happy about it. Warmer weather is bringing many benefits to the Greenland town of Ilulissat.

_____ **A.** one eco-tourist's experience in Ilulissat

_____ **B.** how life in Ilulissat is changing

_____ **C.** when to visit Ilulissat

_____ **D.** the culture and history of Ilulissat

1.2 *Now read the entire article. Use the information to choose the correct answers.*

Global Warming in Ilulissat

Around the world, millions of people are worried about the harsh consequences of global warming. For now, however, there is at least one place that is happy about it. Warmer weather is bringing many benefits to the Greenland town of Ilulissat.

Only 4,500 people inhabit Ilulissat, but 15,000 came to visit in 2007. In 2008, more than 30,000 tourists are expected. Many of the tourists are political leaders who are coming to see global warming occur. Ilulissat is home to many glaciers, which are quickly melting. Political leaders from a variety of countries come to see the glaciers. These leaders want to send the message that they care about the environment. Recent visitors have included the prime minister of Italy and the chancellor of Germany. Other eco-tourists come to see beautiful blue icebergs pass by the coast and the scenic landscape. Now, the town's economy is growing very quickly. There are many new hotels and tour companies, and plenty of jobs.

Global warming is having some positive effects on the local environment as well. As the glaciers become smaller, there is more land for people to live on. The warmer temperatures are making it easier to grow food as well. "The potatoes are big, fresh and tasty," says Buuti Pedersen, a fifty-two-year-old artist. "I could buy broccoli in the shops for the first time." The fishing industry is also benefiting, as warmer waters attract more and more fish. Ilulissat residents are noticing more flowers and new types of birds in their area.

Not everyone is excited, however. Minik Rosing is an environmental scientist. He points out that more people traveling to Greenland will create more pollution and increase global warming. He worries that people in the north of Greenland will lose their traditional way of life as the ice disappears. "Loss of cultural identity and economic benefits are two different categories. You can't quantify the loss of our traditions. The real problem is that we are having to adapt so quickly," he says.

Check (✔) the best answer to complete each sentence.

1. Global warming is benefiting Ilulissat's _____.

    _____ **A.** culture and environment

    _____ **B.** environment and economy

    _____ **C.** economy and government

    _____ **D.** government and culture

2. Politicians come to Ilulissat to _____.

    _____ **A.** show they care about global warming

    _____ **B.** see the beautiful blue icebergs

    _____ **C.** study the loss of cultural traditions

    _____ **D.** meet with Greenland's farmers

3. Ten years ago, it was probably difficult to _____ in Ilulissat.

    _____ **A.** see icebergs

    _____ **B.** work as a scientist

    _____ **C.** find broccoli

    _____ **D.** follow traditions

1.3 *Check (✔) the two things that Minik Rosing is worried about.*

    _____ the health of his neighbors

    _____ the chancellor of Germany

    _____ loss of traditions

    _____ pollution from tourism

    _____ losing his job

1.4   *Read the passage from "Tourists in a Fragile Land" in* NorthStar: Reading and Writing 3, *Unit 5. Use the information from this reading and "Global Warming in Ilulissat" to complete the activity. The first one has been done for you.*

Tourists in a Fragile Land

As a scientist working in Antarctica, I spend most of my time in the lab studying ice. Today, as with an increasing number of days, I had to leave my work to greet a group of tourists who were taking a vacation in this continent of ice. And even though I can appreciate their desire to experience this vast and beautiful landscape, I feel Antarctica should be closed to tourists.

When tourist groups come here, they take us away from our research. Our work is difficult, and some of our projects can be damaged by such simple mistakes as opening the wrong door or bumping into a small piece of equipment. In addition, tourists in Antarctica can also hurt the environment. Members of Greenpeace, one of the world's leading environmental organizations, complain that tourists leave trash on beaches and disturb the plants and animals. In a place as frozen as Antarctica, it can take 100 years for a plant to grow back, and tourists can easily damage penguin eggs. Oil spills are another problem caused by tourism. Oil spills not only kill penguins but can also destroy scientific projects.

If we don't protect Antarctica from tourism, there may be serious consequences for us all. We might lose the results of scientific research projects. It's possible that these results could teach us something important about the causes and effects of climate change. Some fragile plants and animals might die and disappear forever. This could damage the balance of animal and plant life in Antarctica. We know from past experience that when things get unbalanced, harmful changes can occur. Clearly, Antarctica should remain a place for careful and controlled scientific research. We cannot allow tourism to bring possible danger to the planet. The only way to protect this fragile and important part of the planet is to stop tourists from traveling to Antarctica.

Statement	Scientist in Antarctica	Minik Rosing	Both
He studies the environment.			✓
1. He has noticed an increase in tourism.			
2. He is worried about a loss of traditions.			
3. He is worried about pollution from tourism.			
4. Tourists interrupt his work.			

PART 2: VOCABULARY

2.1 *Check (✔) the adjectives that can complete the sentences so they make sense. There are two correct adjectives in number 1 and three correct adjectives in number 2.*

1. Ilulissat is a _____ town of 4,500 people.

   _____ scientific   _____ beautiful

   _____ vast   _____ coastal

   _____ frozen

2. Antarctica is a _____ continent.

   _____ scientific   _____ beautiful

   _____ vast   _____ coastal

   _____ frozen

2.2 *Check (✔) the word closest in meaning to each boldfaced word. There is only one right answer for each item.*

1. **remote**

   _____ **A.** far   _____ **C.** harsh

   _____ **B.** vast   _____ **D.** gentle

2. **researcher**

   _____ **A.** tourist   _____ **C.** artist

   _____ **B.** scientist   _____ **D.** farmer

3. **fragile**

   _____ **A.** frozen   _____ **C.** harsh

   _____ **B.** protected   _____ **D.** delicate

4. **landscape**

   _____ **A.** environment   _____ **C.** harmful changes

   _____ **B.** features of an area   _____ **D.** habitat

5. **inhabit**

   _____ **A.** explore   _____ **C.** preserve

   _____ **B.** change   _____ **D.** live

PART 3: SKILLS FOR WRITING

3.1 *Combine the sentences using* even though *or* because.

1. Scientists live in Antarctica. They want to study the ice there.

   _____

2. Tourism causes pollution. Minik Rosing doesn't want more tourists in Ilulissat.

   _____

3. The flowers in Ilulissat are beautiful. They are a sign of global warming.

   _____

4. Travel to Ilulissat is very expensive. I still want to visit Ilulissat.

   _____

5. Global warming has serious consequences. Scientists are worried.

   _____

3.2 *Read the passage. Use the details from the box to fill in the blanks. Not all of the details will be used.*

covered by ice	research is interrupted by tourism
increased pollution	~~doubled in the last ten years~~
the huge glaciers	the two luxury hotels that opened last year
25 percent of residents	warmer weather makes travel there easier

Tourism has increased to Svalbard, Norway. It has

_____doubled in the last ten years_____. Svalbard is a group of islands in the Arctic

Ocean. Until ten years ago, the islands were _____. The
                                                              1.

main reason tourism is increasing is _____. Tourists
                                                         2.

like the natural beauty of Svalbard, such as _____. One
                                                                  3.

consequence of increased tourism is more construction. Now there are many new

buildings, like _____. Tourism is very important for the
                              4.

local economy. In fact, _____ in Svalbard work in the
                                      5.

tourist industry.

PART 4: WRITING

An Opinion Essay (20 minutes)

Reread "Global Warming in Ilulissat." Then write a three-paragraph essay about tourism in Ilulissat.

- Say if tourists should or shouldn't be allowed to come to Ilulissat.
- Explain your opinion clearly in the beginning of the essay.
- Give at least two reasons to support your opinion.
- Give facts, examples, and explanations to support the reasons. Use information from the reading in Part 1.2.
- Restate the main idea at the end of your essay.
- Use the vocabulary and grammar from Unit 5.

Unit 5 Vocabulary Words						
beauty	effect	frozen	icebergs	natural	research	temperature
coastal	environment	glaciers	inhabit	preserve	scenic	tourists
consequences	fragile	harsh	landscape	remote	scientific	vast

Unit 5 Grammar: *Because* and *Even though*
• Tourism causes pollution *because* tourists leave trash everywhere. • *Even though* tourism helps the economy, tourists often cause pollution.

Achievement Tests
Unit 6

Name: _____

Date: _____

PART 1: READING

1.1 *Read the passage about Hans Christian Andersen. Check (✔) the best prediction of what the reading is about. There is only one right answer.*

The children's stories of Danish author Hans Christian Andersen are in more than 100 languages. They are known by millions of people. During his lifetime, Andersen was one of the most famous authors in Europe. He was also a frequent guest of kings and queens. Shortly before his death, critic Georg Brandes asked Andersen if he would write his life story. Andersen replied that he already had—*The Ugly Duckling*.

_____ **A.** Andersen's travels   _____ **C.** Andersen's other stories

_____ **B.** Andersen's life   _____ **D.** Andersen's death

1.2 *Now read the entire article. Use the information to choose the correct answers.*

Andersen as the Ugly Duckling

The children's stories of Danish author Hans Christian Andersen are in more than 100 languages. They are known by millions of people. During his lifetime, Andersen was one of the most famous authors in Europe. He was also a frequent guest of kings and queens. Shortly before his death, critic Georg Brandes asked Andersen if he would write his life story. Andersen replied that he already had—*The Ugly Duckling*.

The story is considered Andersen's most famous work. In it, a mother duck proudly gives birth to seven baby ducklings. One duckling, however, is the wrong size and color. The other animals all laugh at the duckling. Then he decides to leave the farm. The duckling passes through a terrifying fall and winter, which he barely manages to survive. The duck believes no one will ever love him. The next spring, the lonely duckling meets a group of swans.[1] The swans warmly welcome the duckling. Surprised, the duckling looks at his reflection in the water. He realizes that he, too, is a beautiful swan.

The story of *The Ugly Duckling* has many similarities to Andersen's life. Author Anne Chisholm wrote that Andersen "was a tall, ugly boy with a big nose and big feet." He came from a poor family. Andersen hated school and was often beaten up by his classmates. He felt disgusting and different from others. During these dark years, the only thing that soothed Andersen was time he spent alone, reading.

Andersen's troubles continued into adulthood. Even as he published his first books, he struggled in relationships and doubted himself. For many, many years, Andersen felt as if no one loved him. This feeling made his eventual fame that much more surprising and enjoyable for him.

The moral of *The Ugly Duckling* is that inner beauty and ability are always more important than physical beauty and popularity. Certainly, the success of Hans Christian Andersen shows this to be true.

_____

[1] **swan:** a big white bird with a long neck that lives on lakes and rivers

Check (✔) the best answer to complete each sentence.

1. Georg Brandes was _____.

    _____ **A.** the king of Denmark

    _____ **B.** a friend of Andersen's

    _____ **C.** a critic

    _____ **D.** a writer

2. *The Ugly Duckling* is considered Andersen's _____ story.

    _____ **A.** oldest

    _____ **B.** most famous

    _____ **C.** funniest

    _____ **D.** most serious

3. The fact that the duckling is the wrong size and color is probably based on Andersen's feeling _____.

    _____ **A.** ugly

    _____ **B.** lonely

    _____ **C.** unsuccessful

    _____ **D.** short

4. In *The Ugly Duckling*, the duckling's experiences during the fall and winter are probably based on _____.

    _____ **A.** Andersen's opinion of Denmark

    _____ **B.** Andersen's experiences in school

    _____ **C.** Andersen's publishing his first books

    _____ **D.** Andersen's meeting kings and queens

5. The best title for this article is "The _____ of Hans Christian Andersen."

    _____ **A.** Children's Stories

    _____ **B.** Fame

    _____ **C.** Metamorphosis

    _____ **D.** Complete History

1.3 *Read the passage from "Ungeziefer" in* NorthStar: Reading and Writing 3, *Unit 6.*
*Use the information from this reading and "Andersen as the Ugly Duckling" to complete
the activity. Not all of the details will be used. The first one has been done for you.*

Ungeziefer

Why did Kafka choose to tell a story about a man who turns into a cockroach?
Certainly many people are afraid—even terrified—of cockroaches and other
insects. They think cockroaches are ugly and disgusting. Why would Kafka choose
something that most of us hate? What was his purpose?

One explanation comes from a word that Kafka used in his story. Kafka wrote
his story in German, and he used the German word *ungeziefer,* or vermin,[1] which
can be used to mean a person who is rough and disgusting. In English, we do the
same thing. If we call a person a "cockroach," we mean that the person is weak and
cowardly.[2] Gregor, the man, is like a cockroach. He is weak and disgusting. Why?
Because he doesn't want to be the supporter of his family. He hates his job and
wishes he didn't have to do it in order to pay off the family debt.

Another explanation comes from Kafka's relationship with his father. Kafka was
a small, quiet man. He saw himself as weak compared to his father, who was
physically large and had a powerful personality. It is the same with Gregor. He also
sees himself as a failure. By turning himself into an insect, Gregor is able to rebel
against his father and, at the same time, punish himself for rebelling. This
punishment results in his being physically and emotionally separated from his
family with no hope of joining them again, and finally he dies.

Kafka's choice of an insect makes this story work because many people feel
insects are disgusting. Gregor becomes the vermin, the disgusting son that nobody
cares about. His family rejects him because of his appearance, yet he continues to
love them to the end.

---

[1] **vermin:** small, wild animals, like rats, that can carry diseases and are difficult to control
[2] **cowardly:** afraid, easily frightened

Details

- Andersen met kings and queens.
- Andersen felt ugly.
- Andersen was a swan on the inside.
- Gregor hates his job.

- Andersen's stories are printed in more than 100 languages.
- Kafka saw himself as weak.
- Gregor is like a cockroach.
- ~~Kafka originally wrote in German~~.

Main Idea	Details	
	"Ungeziefer"	"Andersen as the Ugly Duckling"
The works of famous authors are in many languages.	Kafka originally wrote in German.	3.
Some authors have negative opinions of themselves.	1.	4.
Some authors compare people to animals or insects.	2.	5.

PART 2: VOCABULARY

2.1 *Read a passage from* The Ugly Duckling. *Use the words from the box to fill in the blanks. Not all of the words will be used.*

awful	certainly	grabbed	smelly	substance
brave	faint	managed to	soothe	wept

It was a dark and scary night. The ugly duckling was terrified. He wanted to find a

place to sleep. He saw a house. He told himself to be _____. He went into

1.

the house, and suddenly an old woman _____ him. She said, "I'm going to

2.

make you fat, then I'll cook you for dinner!" She put the ugly duckling in a cage. She

fed him a strange _____ he did not recognize. It tasted _____,

3.   4.

but the ugly duckling was so hungry he ate it anyway. This continued for days. The

ugly duckling stopped eating. He thought, "_____, I will die in this house."
_{5.}

Then, one day, the woman forgot to lock the cage, and the ugly duckling

_____ escape.
_{6.}

2.2 *Write the letter of the synonym for the words on the left. Not all of the synonyms will be used.*

_____ 1. weep   **A.** stinky

_____ 2. smelly   **B.** brave

_____ 3. awful   **C.** realize

_____ 4. understand   **D.** cry

                       E. soothe

                       F. very bad

                       G. terrible

PART 3: SKILLS FOR WRITING

3.1 *Read the sentences. Check (✔) the four sentences that use the infinitive to tell about purpose.*

_____ I like to read in my free time.

_____ Andersen read books to forget about school.

_____ Andersen learned to speak four languages.

_____ The old woman made the duckling fat to cook it for dinner.

_____ Kafka decided to write about a cockroach.

_____ He chose a cockroach to disgust people.

_____ Many authors write books to teach morals.

3.2 *Read the paragraph. Notice the underlined words. Use the words from the box to make the underlined words more interesting. Not all of the words in the box will be used.*

brave	cold	excitedly	vastly
breathtaking	delicate	loudly	warm

I woke up in the small cabin. The boat's captain had _____ <u>sounded</u>
1.

the horn. I opened the window, and saw the _____ <u>view</u>. I saw the
2.

_____ <u>sunlight</u> shine on the tall buildings. Coming to the city would
3.

change my life. I _____ <u>grabbed</u> my bag. I went up to the top of the
4.

boat and felt the _____ <u>wind</u> on my face.
5.

PART 4: WRITING

A Story with a Moral (20 minutes)

Write three paragraphs about a time that changed your life.
- Answer the "5Ws": *who, what, when, where,* and *why.*
- Clearly explain what happened and how you felt.
- Use adjectives and adverbs to add detail.
- Explain what you learned from the experience.
- Use the vocabulary and grammar from Unit 6.

Unit 6 Vocabulary Words					
awful	breathtaking	faint	manage to	stinky	ugly
beat up	certainly	fantastic	realize	substance	useless
brave	disgusting	grab	soothe	terrified	weep

Unit 6 Grammar: Infinitives of Purpose
[infinitive] • I went to the station **to buy** a ticket. [infinitive] • I left my home **to start** a new life.

Achievement Tests
Unit 7

Name: _____

Date: _____

PART I: READING

1.1 *Read the story about Samuel Beiler. Check (✔) the best prediction of what Beiler will do. There is only one right answer.*

At the age of seventeen, Samuel Beiler left his Amish community in Lancaster County, Pennsylvania. It was during his *rumspringa,* the period of time when Amish people are free to leave for the outside world. For the next four years, Beiler worked in a factory. He enjoyed the conveniences of modern life and socializing with his new "English" friends. At the same time, however, Beiler felt he could do more with his time on earth. Beiler joined the Peace Corps and went to Honduras as a volunteer. In Honduras, he learned Spanish and worked in a hospital as a translator. He realized that working in a hospital made him happy.

_____ **A.** study to become a doctor   _____ **C.** find a new factory job

_____ **B.** translate for the Amish   _____ **D.** learn to speak French

1.2 *Now read the entire article. Use the information to choose the correct answers.*

A Decision to Return

At the age of seventeen, Samuel Beiler left his Amish community in Lancaster County, Pennsylvania. It was during his *rumspringa,* the period of time when Amish people are free to leave for the outside world. For the next four years, Beiler worked in a factory. He enjoyed the conveniences of modern life and socializing with his new "English" friends. At the same time, however, Beiler felt he could do more with his time on earth. Beiler joined the Peace Corps and went to Honduras as a volunteer. In Honduras, he learned Spanish, and worked in a hospital as a translator. He realized that working in a hospital made him happy.

When Beiler returned to the United States, he decided to study medicine. He had only an eighth-grade education and had never been to high school. Beiler studied hard and was able to receive a high school equivalency diploma and apply to college. In his application, he wrote "Can a person who grew up without electricity, cars, TV, or radio, with only an eighth-grade education, become a doctor? I think the answer is yes." Beiler went to college and then was accepted by the Pittsburgh School of Medicine, where he is now a student.

People are often surprised to learn that Beiler is going to return to his Amish community after he graduates. "My family's church isn't as pious as others," he says. "Because I left during my *rumspringa,* and not after baptism, they are allowing me to return." Beiler plans to establish a doctor's office in his hometown. The decision to return opened up a can of worms for Beiler. On one hand, he would be able to maintain his bond with his family and traditional way of life, while serving his community. On the other hand, he would lose many of the conveniences of modern life he had come to enjoy. "The deciding factor was the community warmly inviting me to return," Beiler says. "I just knew it was the right thing to do."

Check (✔) the best answer to complete each sentence.

1. Beiler worked _____ in Honduras.

   _____ **A.** in a factory

   _____ **B.** in an English school

   _____ **C.** as a doctor

   _____ **D.** as a translator

2. Beiler probably joined the Peace Corps because he wanted to

   _____.

   _____ **A.** make more money

   _____ **B.** visit Honduras

   _____ **C.** help other people

   _____ **D.** study Spanish

3. Now, Beiler probably feels _____ about his decision to leave at

   age seventeen.

   _____ **A.** regretful

   _____ **B.** calm

   _____ **C.** worried

   _____ **D.** happy

4. Beiler's Amish community is allowing him to return because

   _____.

   _____ **A.** he left during *rumspringa*

   _____ **B.** they are very pious

   _____ **C.** he apologized for leaving

   _____ **D.** they need a doctor

5. For Beiler, the decision to return to the Amish community _____.

   _____ **A.** has pros and cons

   _____ **B.** is very convenient

   _____ **C.** has financial benefits

   _____ **D.** is up in the air

1.3 *Read the passage from "A Decision to Leave" in* Northstar: Reading and Writing 3, *Unit 7. Use the information from this reading and "A Decision to Return" to complete the activity. The first one has been done for you.*

A Decision to Leave

As a boy growing up on an Amish farm, Isaac Schlabach became determined not to live as his parents did, struggling all day with labor and chores for very little financial reward. Two weeks before his baptism, which would mark his commitment to the Amish way of life, he decided to leave his family and friends for an uncertain life in the outside world. His older brother had already left, and Isaac knew that he would face a lifetime of regret if he did not try, at least once, to see what life was like in the world of television, cars, and computers. In the back of his mind, he was secure in the knowledge that if he wanted to return to the farm, there would always be a place for him.

He left a simple note for his parents, wishing to avoid their shock and tears. As a 17-year-old, he was eager to test his skill in a world of opportunity. Looking ahead, he decided to invest in real estate with his brother, hoping to achieve financial security for the rest of his life. The two moved to Texas and managed to buy a house. They gradually acquired more and more houses, which brought them rental income and allowed them to continue investing.

Today Isaac works full-time, attends college, and manages his properties. He has found a busy and satisfying life in a world that he had been taught to believe was dangerous and evil. Looking back on his Amish childhood, he recognizes the value of his upbringing, which included hard physical work and neighborly concern for others. He also appreciates the fact that his parents never argued in front of their 14 children, despite all the stresses of raising a large family on a limited budget. His only regret is the loss of contact with his Amish relatives, especially his mother, whom he contacts once or twice a year. At the same time, he enjoys all the rewards that have come as a result of his success in the modern world of business.

Statement	Isaac Schlabach	Samuel Beiler	Both
He left home at age seventeen.			✓
1. He attends college / graduate school.			
2. He plans to return to the Amish community.			
3. He regrets the lack of contact with family.			
4. He likes the modern world.			

PART 2: VOCABULARY

2.1 *Read the story. Use the words from the box to fill in the blanks. Not all of the words will be used.*

allowed	bonds	pious	socialize
be stuck between a rock and a hard place	declined	pros and cons	turn him down
	persecution		

For a long time, Samuel Beiler was up in the air about whether he wanted to return

home or not. He had so many doubts. What if he wasn't _____ to
                                                                1.

return? Was it possible the community would _____ when he asked
                                                            2.

to come back? Also, if he went back, would he experience _____
                                                                        3.

from people who were angry that he had left in the first place? If he returned home

and regretted it, he would really _____: unhappy at home, but not
                                                    4.

wanting to leave a second time. Beiler carefully considered the _____
                                                                                5.

of his situation. In the end, he decided to rejoin his community.

2.2 *Cross out the vocabulary item in each group that does not relate to the others.*

1. maintain   allow   continue   keep

2. turn down   benefit   decline   refuse

3. allow   permit   establish   accept

4. pious   bond   connection   closeness

5. establish   begin   decline   start

PART 3: SKILLS FOR WRITING

3.1 *Complete the responses with noun clauses with* wh- *words. Use the same subject, main verb, and* wh- *word as the question. You may need to change the verb to agree with the subject.*

Q: Who are the Amish?
R: In school, I'm learning _____ *who the Amish are.* _____

1. **Q:** Where do the Amish live?
   R: Here, this map shows _____

2. **Q:** What does *rumspringa* mean?
   R: Sorry, I can't remember _____

3. **Q:** How do Amish people dress?
   R: Look, this photo shows _____

4. **Q:** Are there Amish communities in New York state?
   R: Honestly, I'm not sure _____

5. **Q:** Do the Amish play sports?
   R: Actually, I don't know _____

3.2 *Use parallel structure to combine each pair of sentences. You may need to change the verb to agree with the subject.*

1. The Amish like to live a traditional life.
   The Amish like to avoid modern technology.

   _____

2. For the Amish, religion is very important.
   For the Amish, family is very important.

   _____

3. Samuel Beiler was raised in an Amish community.
   Isaac Schlabach was raised in an Amish community.

   _____

4. When I have enough free time, I'll visit Amish country.
   When I have enough extra money, I'll visit Amish country.

   _____

5. Amish teenagers may leave the community during *rumspringa*.
   Amish teenagers may stay during *rumspringa*.

   _____

PART 4: WRITING

An Explanation of a Decision (20 minutes)

Reread the story about Samuel Beiler in "A Decision to Return." Then write a three-paragraph letter from Samuel to his parents, explaining his decision to leave.

- Pretend you are Samuel Beiler at age seventeen. Use first person ("I").
- In the first paragraph, tell your parents that you are leaving and that it is a very difficult decision.
- In the following paragraphs, explain the pros and cons of your decision. Discuss one topic in each paragraph.
- Use noun clauses with *wh-* words and parallel structure when possible.
- Use the vocabulary and grammar from Unit 7.

Unit 7 Vocabulary Words					
allowed	deciding factor	maintain	pious	stuck between	the pros and cons
bonds	decline	open up a can	settle down	a rock and	turn (him) down
conveniences	establish	of worms	socialize	a hard place	up in the air

Unit 7 Grammar: Noun Clauses with *Wh-* Words
• My father asked **why I want to leave.** • I want to know **what the world is like.**

Achievement Tests
Unit 8

Name: _____

Date: _____

PART 1: READING

1.1   *Read the beginning of an interview with a matchmaker. Check (✔) the best description of Selma Wilcott. There is only one right answer.*

BRIDE MAGAZINE: So what is your background?

SELMA WILCOTT: I have a degree in psychology and fifteen years of experience helping people find a marriage partner.

_____ **A.** romantic   _____ **C.** traditional

_____ **B.** knowledgeable   _____ **D.** unique

1.2   *Now read the entire interview. Use the information to choose the correct answers.*

Why Hire a Matchmaker?

BRIDE MAGAZINE: So what is your background?

SELMA WILCOTT: I have a degree in psychology and fifteen years of experience helping people find a marriage partner.

BRIDE MAGAZINE: Why should people pay a matchmaker to find them a spouse?

SELMA WILCOTT: Well, when you meet someone at work, or at a party, often the first thing connecting you to that person is physical attraction or something simple you have in common. It is unlikely that everlasting love will come out of that situation. It does sometimes, but that is usually by chance. More often it ends with someone having a broken heart. When you work with a matchmaker, you can avoid a lot of that.

BRIDE MAGAZINE: How do you help your clients?

SELMA WILCOTT: First, I interview the person and decide what characteristics he or she needs in a spouse. This is where my background in psychology is important. After that, I start looking for the perfect match, and when I have a good one, I introduce them.

BRIDE MAGAZINE: How often are your matches successful?

SELMA WILCOTT: I'm proud of my work—more than 70 percent of my clients become engaged after they work with me.

BRIDE MAGAZINE: That's impressive. Some people say going to a matchmaker isn't romantic. What do you think about that?

SELMA WILCOTT: Falling in love with the right person will always be romantic, no matter how and where you meet each other.

BRIDE MAGAZINE: Last question—what is your opinion of arranged marriage?

SELMA WILCOTT: *(laughs)* Well, some people think it isn't modern, but in truth, it produces a lot of happy couples. Really, it isn't that different from what I do here.

Check (✔) the best answer to complete each sentence.

1. Selma thinks paying a matchmaker is better than _____.

    _____ A. having an arranged marriage

    _____ B. finding a spouse on the Internet

    _____ C. being romantic

    _____ D. meeting someone at work or at a bar

2. Selma matches people based on their _____.

    _____ A. lifestyles

    _____ B. characteristics

    _____ C. backgrounds

    _____ D. attractiveness

3. Selma probably thinks physical attraction is _____ for a happy marriage.

    _____ A. more important than having similar lifestyles

    _____ B. less important than having similar careers

    _____ C. more important than having similar backgrounds

    _____ D. less important than having similar characteristics

4. Overall, Selma thinks her matchmaking service is very _____.

    _____ A. successful

    _____ B. romantic

    _____ C. modern

    _____ D. convenient

5. Most of Selma's clients get _____ after they work with her.

    _____ A. a degree

    _____ B. an arranged marriage

    _____ C. engaged

    _____ D. a broken heart

1.3 *Read "What's Wrong with Tradition?" from* Northstar: Reading and Writing 3, *Unit 8. Use the information from this reading and "Why Hire a Matchmaker?" to complete the activity. The first one has been done for you.*

What's Wrong with Tradition?

Dear Editor:

I am a twenty-seven-year-old student from Vietnam. My purpose in coming here is to get a business degree. I am very grateful to have the chance to get an education in a country of such great business leadership. However, I am tired of the questions that people ask me about my personal life. American students seem to think that their way of dating romantically before marriage is the only way, but I disagree. Let me give you an example from my own life.

My parents have been married for thirty-five years. Their marriage has all the characteristics of a happy one: deep friendship, love, and trust. They have six children, and I am the second son. Because of their help, I am able to study in the United States. They have always worked hard to raise their children in the right way. When I finish my degree, I will go back to my country and help them.

American people are always surprised when I tell them that my parents met for the first time on their wedding day. Americans can't believe that an arranged marriage could be happy, but I have seen my parents with my own eyes. They love each other faithfully, and they are proud of the children that their marriage has produced. They learned to love each other slowly, as time passed. I believe they share a true and everlasting love.

When people ask, "Are you looking for a girlfriend?" I tell them no. For me, studying comes first. When I go back to my country and start working, my parents will help me find a good wife. She will be someone with a good family background, someone I can trust. Good apples come from good trees. If I marry a good apple, we can make a beautiful, growing tree together: no divorce, no AIDS, no broken heart.

I want a peaceful, happy life just like my parents have. Why can't Americans understand this?

Paul Nguyen

Statement	Paul Nguyen	Selma Wilcott	Both
He / she thinks dating is often a waste of time.			✓
1. He / she has a university degree now.			
2. He / she has a positive opinion of arranged marriage.			
3. He / she wants to avoid broken hearts.			
4. He / she thinks parents choose the best spouses.			

PART 2: VOCABULARY

2.1 *Read the story. Use the words from the box to fill in the blanks. Not all of the words will be used.*

attracted	custom	faithful	pregnant	surprised
characteristics	engagement	fertility	spouse	unique

Tony and Linda Williams have been married for two years. Instead of a traditional ceremony, Tony and Linda Williams had a "Vegas Wedding." They met at a casino in Las Vegas and were immediately _____ to each other. After spending two
1.

days together, they decided to get married. Their _____ lasted only 30
2.

minutes—the amount of time it took them to drive to a wedding chapel. Their

families were _____ by the news, but happy for the new couple. Now the
3.

Williamses live together in Mesa, Arizona. Linda is _____ with the
4.

couple's first child. "I know our wedding was different," Linda says with a smile.

"But I like that it was _____."
5.

2.2 *Check (✔) the word that best completes each comparison. There is only one right answer for each item.*

1. custom : tradition = spouse : _____

    _____ **A.** fertility

    _____ **B.** engagement

    _____ **C.** partner

    _____ **D.** wedding

2. engagement : marriage = fertility : _____

    _____ **A.** polygamy

    _____ **B.** romance

    _____ **C.** attraction

    _____ **D.** pregnancy

3. leader : follower = everlasting : _____

    _____ **A.** huge

    _____ **B.** short

    _____ **C.** true

    _____ **D.** unique

4. wedding : happy = divorce : _____

    _____ **A.** infertile

    _____ **B.** broken hearted

    _____ **C.** faithful

    _____ **D.** modern

5. features : characteristics = produce : _____

    _____ **A.** make

    _____ **B.** raise

    _____ **C.** stop

    _____ **D.** reduce

PART 3: SKILLS FOR WRITING

3.1 *Read the story. Fill in the blanks with* a *or* the.

Last weekend was so great. I went to __*a*__ wedding. _____ wedding was in Las Vegas.
                                                        1.

It was _____ best wedding I've ever been to. Everybody had so much fun! My friend
          2.

Joe got married. He wore _____ white suit, and it looked great. _____ suit was a gift
                          3.   **4.**

from his parents. After the wedding, everybody went to _____ restaurant. We ate and
                                                        5.

drank all night. What a good time!

3.2 *Read the story. Use the words from the box to fill in the blanks. Not all of the words will be used.*

custom	marriage	similar	surprise
customary	married	similarity	surprising
customize	marry	similarly	surprised

Last week my sister got engaged! The _____ thing is that she is six
                                        1.

years younger than I am. I'm not _____; I don't even have a
                                  2.

boyfriend! _____ is an important thing, and I'm afraid my sister is
            3.

making a mistake. She isn't _____ to the guy at all! Their only
                            4.

_____ is that they both work at the same restaurant. My friends tell
5.

me I am just jealous, but I think this is a bad idea.

PART 4: WRITING

A Descriptive Essay (20 minutes)

Write a four-paragraph essay about the individual and shared interests of a couple you know.

- In the first paragraph, say who the couple is and if they are happy or unhappy together.
- In the first body paragraph, talk about their shared interests; in the second, talk about their individual interests.
- Use details and examples to clearly show your ideas.
- Restate the main idea in your conclusion paragraph.
- Use related word forms as cohesive devices when possible.
- Use the vocabulary and grammar from Unit 8.

Unit 8 Vocabulary Words					
arranged marriage	broken heart	engagement	modern	proud	spouse
attracted to	characteristics	everlasting	pregnant	raise	surprise
background	custom	faithfully	produce	romantic	traditional

Unit 8 Grammar: Definite and Indefinite Articles

[indefinite article]
• They are *a* great couple.

[definite article]
• They are *the* happiest couple I know.

Achievement Tests
Unit 9

Name: _____

Date: _____

PART 1: READING

1.1 *Read the passage about climate change. Check (✔) the best prediction of what the reading is about. There is only one right answer.*

In the words of most scientists, global warming works something like this: Humans burn fossil fuels, which release greenhouse gases into the atmosphere. As a result, the atmosphere becomes thicker and traps more of the sun's energy. Consequently, the Earth gets warmer, and various environmental problems result. If one accepts this explanation, then the problem of climate change begins with the use of fossil fuels.

_____ **A.** using less fossil fuel   _____ **C.** using greenhouse gases

_____ **B.** using the sun's energy   _____ **D.** stopping climate change

1.2 *Now read the entire article. Use the information to choose the correct answers.*

The Fossil Fuel Controversy

In the words of most scientists, global warming works something like this: Humans burn fossil fuels, which release greenhouse gases into the atmosphere. As a result, the atmosphere becomes thicker and traps more of the sun's energy. Consequently, the Earth gets warmer, and various environmental problems result. If one accepts this explanation, then the problem of climate change begins with the use of fossil fuels. Economists, and some scientists as well, have argued that using fossil fuels is a necessary part of modern life. Many scientists disagree and look for ways to reduce humans' use of fossil fuels. One common suggestion is to make cars that need less fuel to operate. Even this basic suggestion, however, is controversial in the United States.

Supporters of the idea say it would bring both environmental and economic benefits. If cars used less fuel, people would save money by not having to go to the gas station as often. Furthermore, cars would emit less carbon dioxide, a greenhouse gas. Currently, 6 percent of the carbon dioxide released into the atmosphere comes from cars in the United States. Supporters say this number could easily be reduced to 4 percent. Currently, the average car in the United States gets 27 miles per gallon of gas. Now, the technology exists for some cars to get 36 or more miles per gallon. Some people say every car should be required by law to get 36 or more miles per gallon.

Other people are not so sure. They say there is no evidence that carbon dioxide causes global warming. They also argue such rules could make cars too expensive for the average person. According to General Motors Vice Chairman Bob Lutz, following these rules would cost $5,000 to $7,000 more per car. "Technology is an easy thing to do. What's not easy is the cost," Lutz says. Many U.S. carmakers already have serious financial problems, and some economists think they would not survive under the suggested rules.

Environmentalists are quick to disagree with Lutz's opinion. "Everyone has to adapt to climate change," says Marie Lefferts of *Earth First,* an organization that studies climate change. "That includes the car companies."

Check (✔) the best answer to complete each sentence.

1. Most scientists think the origin of global warming is _____.

   _____ **A.** more expensive cars

   _____ **B.** the increasingly thin atmosphere

   _____ **C.** humans' use of fossil fuels

   _____ **D.** heat from the sun's energy

2. Generally, _____ disagree with each other about using less fossil fuel.

   _____ **A.** scientists and politicians

   _____ **B.** politicians and economists

   _____ **C.** economists and environmentalists

   _____ **D.** environmentalists and scientists

3. Today, most cars in the United States get _____ miles per gallon.

   _____ **A.** 36

   _____ **B.** 27

   _____ **C.** 6

   _____ **D.** 17

4. Bob Lutz thinks requiring all cars to get 36 miles per gallon would be

   _____.

   _____ **A.** too expensive

   _____ **B.** too controversial

   _____ **C.** good for the environment

   _____ **D.** good for the economy

5. Marie Lefferts probably thinks carmakers should create _____.

   _____ **A.** more cars that emit carbon dioxide

   _____ **B.** more fuel-efficient cars

   _____ **C.** cars that get fewer miles per gallon

   _____ **D.** cars that cost only $5,000–$7,000

1.3 *Read the passage from "Climate Change: Making Informed Decisions" in* Northstar: Reading and Writing 3, *Unit 9. Use the information from this reading and "The Fossil Fuel Controversy" to complete the activity. The first one has been done for you.*

Climate Change: Making Informed Decisions

For the past decade, there have been angry debates over whether our planet is heating up and whose fault it is. Clearly, the experts can't agree. So, what is the average person supposed to think, or do, about this issue?

Can carbon dioxide produced by humans cause climate change? In 1988, a group of scientists called the International Panel on Climate Change (IPCC) met to discuss three critical issues: 1) how our lifestyles affect the Earth's climate, 2) how climate change would affect us in the future, and 3) how exactly to deal with climate change. Later, the IPCC recommendations were used to write the Kyoto Protocol, a 1997 agreement that addressed our role in the Earth's changing atmosphere and set international limits for gas emissions.

A few governments, including the United States and Saudi Arabia, and some companies don't support the Kyoto Protocol. They think achieving the limits recommended by the Protocol would cost too much money and be bad for business. Scientists retained[1] by these governments and companies argue that recent climate change is not actually caused by humans. These scientists don't think we really need to change our lifestyles, that is, we should continue to drive, fly, and live normally. They present evidence they say proves that the Earth is going through a normal heating and cooling cycle, as it has done throughout its history.

So, is there a link between humans and climate change or not? Who should we believe? The IPCC or the governments and companies that disagree with it? To reach an educated opinion, it is important to think about the people who make scientific claims and what their purposes may be.

And what about the other experts who say our use of fossil fuels is *not* causing climate change? Well, some of *them* receive money from companies that produce these fossil fuels. For example, ExxonMobil, one of the world's biggest oil companies, spends $2 million a year to support groups that discredit[2] the idea of global warming. When we hear reports on climate change, we must use good judgment and ask ourselves where the facts are coming from. We must interpret the research, make informed decisions, and most importantly, continue to actively participate in the debate.

---

[1] **retained:** paid to work for a company now and in the future

[2] **discredit:** to criticize people or things so that they are not respected

Statement	"Climate Change: Making Informed Decisions"	"The Fossil Fuel Controversy"	Both
Scientists have a lot to say about the debate over the causes of climate change.			✓
1. Climate change problems are caused by fossil fuels.			
2. Cars that use less fuel would be good for the environment and the economy.			
3. The experts cannot agree about the causes of climate change.			
4. The Earth is going through a normal heating and cooling cycle.			
5. Limits and rules about the use of fossil fuels could cost a lot of money.			

PART 2: VOCABULARY

2.1 *Check (✔) the adjectives that can complete the sentences so they make sense. There are two correct adjectives in number 1 and three correct adjectives in number 2.*

1. Climate change is a(n) _____ problem for our planet.

    _____ successful   _____ energetic   _____ obvious   _____ massive

    _____ warm   _____ national   _____ thick

2. Scientists say carbon dioxide results in a _____ atmosphere.

    _____ successful   _____ energetic   _____ obvious   _____ massive

    _____ warm   _____ national   _____ thick

2.2 *Read the passage. Use the words from the box to fill in the blanks. Not all of the words will be used.*

adapts	emit	escapes	gas	link
atmosphere	energetic	evidence	limit	signs

Many famous actors such as George Clooney and Leonardo DiCaprio have spoken about how humans create climate change. They urge Americans to _____ their

1.
use of fossil fuels. One famous American disagrees, however. Michael Crichton, author of books such as *Jurassic Park* and *Sphere*, doubts there is any _____

2.
between human activity and global warming. In his 2004 novel *State of Fear*, a group of terrorists create natural disasters to make the public believe they are

_____ of global warming. Characters in the book say there is little to no

3.
_____ for global warming. In the end, the hero _____ from the "eco-

4.   5.
terrorists" and stops them. Many scientists say the book is ridiculous; however, it won an award from the oil industry in 2006 for "excellent journalism."

PART 3: SKILLS FOR WRITING

3.1 *Read the interview with an environmental scientist. Use the words from the box to fill in the blanks. Not all of the words will be used.*

are going to	do you think	~~is it possible~~	might
couldn't	have to	may not	will

Q: So, ____is it possible____ global warming is not really happening?

A: No, it's a reality, and the evidence says that people are responsible for it.

Q: I see. _____ global warming will melt the polar ice caps?

1.

A: Yes, that _____ happen. It's possible.

2.

Q: When _____ it happen? Soon, or not for many years?
     <small>**3.**</small>

A: It _____ happen in our lifetime. Probably 100 years from now.
       <small>**4.**</small>

Q: In the movie *Day After Tomorrow,* it happened in only two days. Is that possible?

A: No, that's impossible. That _____ happen.
                                      <small>**5.**</small>

3.2 *Complete the sentences with the best choice of transitions.*

1. The atmosphere is heating up _____ humans use so much
                                    (since / consequently)
   fossil fuel.

2. Rivers can dry up. _____ we may not have enough water to
                          (As a result, / As)
   drink.

3. Farming would be more difficult, _____ we couldn't water the
                                        (therefore / as)
   crops enough.

4. The problem is serious. _____ we must work together to solve it.
                              (Therefore, / Since)

PART 4: WRITING

Cause-and-Effect Essay (20 minutes)

Write a four-paragraph essay about the idea to require all cars to get 36 miles per gallon.
- In your first paragraph, state the idea and say whether you think it is good or not.
- In the second paragraph, say what the effects will be if everybody follows that rule.
- In the third paragraph, say what the effects will be if people *do not* follow that rule.
- Use causal chains to clearly show your ideas; use transitions to show cause and effect.
- Restate the main idea in the last paragraph.
- Use the vocabulary and grammar from Unit 9.

Unit 9 Vocabulary Words						
adapt	carbon dioxide	emissions	escape	fossil fuels	limited	reduce
atmosphere	climate	energetic	evidence	gases	link	sign

Unit 9 Grammar: Future Possibility: *May, Might, Could*
• Poor people *might not* like this law.
• This law *could* improve air quality.

PART 1: READING

1.1 *Read the passage about Singapore. Check (✔) the best prediction of what the reading is about. There is only one right answer.*

Singapore is a small South-Pacific island nation of four million people. It is often called the "Garden City of Asia." Visitors to the city of Singapore say it is the cleanest city in the world. People say it is one of the safest cities as well. There are very few crimes, and police spend most of their day giving directions. Tourists are often surprised when they discover that Singapore has the highest execution rate per capita in the world.

_____ **A.** Singapore's government   _____ **C.** crime and punishment

_____ **B.** safety tips for tourists   _____ **D.** police activities

1.2 *Now read the entire article. Use the information to choose the correct answers.*

Singapore and the Death Penalty

Singapore is a small South-Pacific island nation of four million people. It is often called the "Garden City of Asia." Visitors to the city of Singapore say it is the cleanest city in the world. People say it is one of the safest cities as well. There are very few crimes, and police spend most of their day giving directions. Tourists are often surprised when they discover that Singapore has the highest execution rate per capita in the world.

Between 1991 and 2001, the government of Singapore executed 340 people. Singapore has only four million citizens and more than thirty executions a year. This city has the highest execution rate in the world compared to its population, according to human rights group Amnesty International.

Many countries that have abolished the death penalty complain to Singapore. They argue that the death penalty teaches revenge instead of forgiveness. In addition, innocent people may be put to death, they say. Singapore has no plans to change its system of justice, however.

"There is widespread belief amongst lawmakers and the public in Singapore that the death penalty has worked," says National University of Singapore law professor Michael Hor. In 2004, the crime rate in Singapore per 100,000 people was 481. In the same year the United States had a crime rate of 3,982 per 100,000. In Singapore, a wide variety of crimes is punishable by death. These crimes include drug possession, use of a gun, and kidnapping. Supporters of the death penalty argue that it helps to prevent all of these crimes. They say the death penalty also helps prevent many smaller crimes, such as theft.

Many citizens of Singapore support the death penalty. For them the question is not whether one has a right to life. The question is what is best for the country as a whole. "Our approach . . . places the interests of the community over and above that of the individual," says Singapore's Senior Minister Lee Kuan Yew.

Check (✔) the best answer to complete each sentence.

1. Visitors describe Singapore as _____ and safe.

    _____ **A.** quiet

    _____ **B.** clean

    _____ **C.** small

    _____ **D.** fun

2. Singapore uses the death penalty, even though _____.

    _____ **A.** it has few crimes punishable by death

    _____ **B.** it has an increasing crime rate

    _____ **C.** most Singaporeans do not support it

    _____ **D.** other countries ask it to stop

3. When Michael Hor says "the death penalty has worked," he means it has

    _____.

    _____ **A.** helped the economy of Singapore

    _____ **B.** led to an increase in tourism

    _____ **C.** resulted in a low crime rate

    _____ **D.** passed many legal challenges

4. Most citizens of Singapore believe their government's use of the death penalty

    is _____.

    _____ **A.** effective

    _____ **B.** controversial

    _____ **C.** unnecessary

    _____ **D.** frequent

5. Lee Kuan Yew probably feels that _____ is more important than

    individual rights.

    _____ **A.** taxpayer money

    _____ **B.** justice for victims

    _____ **C.** a clean city

    _____ **D.** public safety

1.3 *Read the chart from* Northstar: Reading and Writing 3, *Unit 10. Use the information from this chart and "Singapore and the Death Penalty" to complete the activity. The first one has been done for you.*

---

1. **Executions by Country in 2006**

China	$1,010 =$	64%
Iran	$177 =$	11%
Pakistan	$82 =$	5%
Iraq	$65 =$	4%
Sudan	$65 =$	4%
United States	$53 =$	3%
Other[1]		9%

2. **Do you support or oppose capital punishment for murderers?**[2]

Support	65%
Oppose	28%
Undecided	7%

3. **Do you support capital punishment or life imprisonment with absolutely no chance of parole for murderers?**

Support capital punishment	47%
Support life imprisonment with no parole	48%
Undecided	5%

   ---

   [1] This represents the other 62 countries that have capital punishment and use it, but do very few executions as compared with the 6 countries listed above.
   [2] Questions 2 and 3 were asked of Americans.

Statement	The United States	Singapore	Both
It has the death penalty.			✓
1. It executes more than thirty people a year.			
2. It accounts for 3 percent of executions in the world.			
3. Most people in this country support the death penalty for murderers.			
4. Its main concern is the community, not the individual.			

PART 2: VOCABULARY

2.1 *Write the abstract nouns from the box next to the examples that illustrate them. Not all of the abstract nouns will be used.*

forgiveness	justice	respect	trust
innocence	punishment	support	violence

Abstract Noun	Example
	1. A man is sent to prison for ten years.
	2. A woman doesn't commit any crime.
	3. A man shoots another man with a gun.
	4. A victim feels better because the thief is in jail.
	5. A victim accepts a criminal's apology.

2.2 *Write the letter of the synonym for the words on the left. Not all of the synonyms will be used.*

_____ 1. abolish   A. revenge

_____ 2. killer   B. murderer

C. forgive

D. end

E. criminal

2.3 *Write the letter of the antonym (opposite meaning) for the words on the left. Not all of the antonyms will be used.*

_____ 1. innocent   A. fair

_____ 2. cruel   B. respect

_____ 3. support   C. oppose

D. justice

E. guilty

F. violent

PART 3: SKILLS FOR WRITING

3.1 *Read the story. Complete it with the present perfect or the present perfect progressive form of the verbs in parentheses.*

Recently, the state of New Jersey has ended its use of the death penalty. It is the first

state that _____ the death penalty in forty years. Opponents of the
            1. (abolish)

death penalty _____ for this news for a long time. "We always
              2. (wait)

_____ New Jersey would do the right thing," says Rashawn
   3. (believe)

Happermire, twenty-seven. "I _____ here for ten years, and this is
                          4. (be)

the proudest I've ever been of my state." Other states, such as Maryland, Montana,

Nebraska, and New Mexico, _____ New Jersey's case and may abolish
                          5. (watch)

the death penalty as well.

3.2 *Combine each pair of sentences into one compound or complex sentence using the connector in parentheses. Use subject pronouns when possible. You may need to add commas to some sentences.*

1. Singapore has strict laws. Tourists should read about them before they visit. (so)

   _____

2. States give killers the death penalty. States give them life sentences. (or)

   _____

3. The United States has executed 1,099 people. The United States legalized the

   death penalty in 1976. (since)

   _____

4. The death penalty is legal in Brazil. The death penalty is rarely used there.

   (although)

   _____

5. The death penalty is discussed in the United States. There is always

   controversy. (when)

   _____

PART 4: WRITING

A Persuasive Essay (20 minutes)

Reread "Singapore and the Death Penalty." Then write a five-paragraph essay about the death penalty from the point of view of a citizen of Singapore.

- In the first paragraph, state your opinion clearly in a thesis statement.
- In the paragraphs that follow, explain the reasons for your opinion. Include details and examples to clearly show your ideas
- Mention one opposing reason and refute it.
- Restate the main idea in the last paragraph.
- Use a variety of sentence types: simple, compound, and complex.
- Use the vocabulary and grammar from Unit 10.

Unit 10 Vocabulary Words					
abolish	cruel	guilty	murderer	respect	society
citizens	execution	innocent	oppose	revenge	support
criminal	forgiveness	justice	punishment	rights	violent

Unit 10 Grammar: Present Perfect and Present Perfect Progressive
[present perfect]   [present perfect progressive]   • We ***have executed*** many people, and the world ***has been watching.***

Achievement Tests Answer Key

UNIT 1

1.1

B

1.2

1. B   2. C   3. D   4. D   5. C

1.3

1. Billboard advertising is common in China.
2. Advertising used to be illegal in China.
3. Most Chinese consumers don't like cheese.
4. Frito-Lay changed the picture on the *Cheetos* bag from a cartoon cat to a red sun.
5. China prohibited the import of potatoes.

2.1

1. impression   2. succeed   3. competition

2.2

1. campaign
2. caught the eye
3. paid attention
4. commercials
5. catchy
6. message

3.1

1. is experimenting
2. introduces
3. is introducing
4. advertises
5. are increasing
6. think

3.2

1. Frito-Lay is also successful in India.
2. I do not like spicy food very much, so I wouldn't order it!
3. Some British people put corn in sandwiches.
4. In France, people put corn in salads.

PART 4

Answers will vary. See the scoring rubric on page T-69.

UNIT 2

1.1

B

1.2

1. D   2. A   3. C   4. D   5. D

1.3

1. She felt scared and angry.
2. Another woman was calling herself Michelle Brown.
3. Americans lose $200 million a year to fraud.
4. Julia was weary of fishy e-mail offers.
5. A man said he was a rich politician.

2.1

1. suspect
2. suspect
3. suspiciously
4. deceive
5. deceptive
6. deceptively
7. impersonation

2.2

1. impersonating
2. fishy
3. suspicious
4. motive

3.1

1. stole
2. discovered
3. was looking
4. called
5. was talking

3.2

1. C   2. B   3. D

PART 4

Answers will vary. See the scoring rubric on page T-69.

UNIT 3

1.1

C

1.2

1. B   2. B   3. D   4. A   5. C

1.3

1. Both
2. Jesse Marunde
3. Ashley Lindermann
4. Both

2.1

1. escape
2. pressure
3. control
4. benefits
5. hooked on

2.2

1. achievement
2. athletically
3. obsess
4. obsessive
5. beneficial
6. beneficially

3.1

1. can
   is able to
2. couldn't
   wasn't able to

3.2

1. ONDCP
2. stacking
3. pyramiding
4. Frederickson
5. a study

PART 4

Answers will vary. See the scoring rubric on page T-69.

UNIT 4

1.1

A

1.2

1. C   2. B   3. D   4. B   5. B

1.3

1. They use fewer commands.
2. Husbands and wives annoy each other.
3. Men want to achieve status.
4. They don't interrupt as often.
5. Women want to say more, but don't.

2.1

1. the dirt   6. feminine
2. juicy   7. emphasized
3. bluntly   8. rough and tough
4. gender   9. status
5. influences   10. compete

3.1

1. more frequently than   3. as directly as
2. less competitively than   4. as patiently as

3.2

1. however   2. unlike
   on the other hand   in contrast to
   in contrast

PART 4

Answers will vary. See the scoring rubric on page T-69.

UNIT 5

1.1

B

1.2

1. B   2. A   3. C

1.3

loss of traditions
pollution from tourism

1.4

1. Both   3. Both
2. Minik Rosing   4. Scientist in Antarctica

2.1

1. beautiful   2. vast
   coastal   frozen
                           beautiful

2.2

1. A   2. B   3. D   4. B   5. D

3.1

1. Scientists live in Antarctica because they want to study the ice there. OR
   Because they want to study the ice there, scientists live in Antarctica.
2. Minik Rosing doesn't want more tourists in Ilulissat because tourism causes pollution. OR
   Because tourism causes pollution, Minik Rosing doesn't want more tourists in Ilulissat.
3. The flowers in Ilulissat are beautiful even though they are a sign of global warming. OR
   Even though they are a sign of global warming, the flowers in Ilulissat are beautiful.
4. I still want to visit Ilulissat even though travel to Ilulissat is very expensive. OR
   Even though travel to Ilulissat is very expensive, I still want to visit Ilulissat.
5. Scientists are worried because global warming has serious consequences. OR
   Because global warming has serious consequences, scientists are worried.

3.2

1. covered by ice
2. warmer weather makes travel there easier
3. the huge glaciers
4. the two luxury hotels that opened last year
5. 25 percent of residents

PART 4

Answers will vary. See the scoring rubric on page T-69.

UNIT 6

1.1

B

1.2

1. C   2. B   3. A   4. B   5. C

1.3

1. Kafka saw himself as weak.
2. Gregor is like a cockroach.
3. Andersen's stories are printed in more than 100 languages.
4. Andersen felt ugly.
5. Andersen was a swan on the inside.

2.1

| 1. brave | 3. substance | 5. Certainly |
| 2. grabbed | 4. awful | 6. managed to |

2.2

1. D   2. A   3. G   4. C

3.1

1. Andersen read books to forget about school.
2. The old woman made the duckling fat to cook it for dinner.
3. He chose a cockroach to disgust people.
4. Many authors write books to teach morals.

3.2

| 1. loudly | 3. warm | 5. cold |
| 2. breathtaking | 4. excitedly | |

PART 4

Answers will vary. See the scoring rubric on page T-69.

UNIT 7

1.1

A

1.2

1. D   2. C   3. D   4. A   5. A

1.3

| 1. Both | 3. Isaac Schlabach |
| 2. Samuel Beiler | 4. Both |

2.1

1. allowed
2. turn him down
3. persecution
4. be stuck between a rock and a hard place
5. pros and cons

2.2

| 1. allow | 3. establish | 5. decline |
| 2. benefit | 4. pious | |

3.1

1. where the Amish live.
2. what *rumspringa* means.
3. how Amish people dress.
4. if / whether there are Amish communities in New York state.
5. if / whether the Amish play sports.

3.2

1. The Amish like to live a traditional life and avoid modern technology. OR
   The Amish like to avoid modern technology and live a traditional life.
2. For the Amish, religion and family are very important. OR
   For the Amish, family and religion are very important.
3. Samuel Beiler and Isaac Schlabach were raised in Amish communities. OR
   Isaac Schlabach and Sameul Beiler were raised in Amish communities.
4. When I have enough free time and extra money, I'll visit Amish country. OR
   When I have enough extra money and free time, I'll visit Amish country.
5. Amish teenagers may leave the community or stay during *rumspringa*. OR
   Amish teenagers may stay or leave the community during *rumspringa*.

PART 4

Answers will vary. See the scoring rubric on page T-69.

UNIT 8

1.1

B

1.2

1. D   2. B   3. D   4. A   5. C

1.3

| 1. Selma Wilcott | 3. Both |
| 2. Both | 4. Paul Nguyen |

2.1

| 1. attracted | 3. surprised | 5. unique |
| 2. engagement | 4. pregnant | |

2.2

1. C   2. D   3. B   4. B   5. A

3.1

1. The   2. the   3. a   4. The   5. a

3.2

| 1. surprising | 3. Marriage | 5. similarity |
| 2. married | 4. similar | |

PART 4

Answers will vary. See the scoring rubric on page T-69.

UNIT 9

1.1

A

1.2

1. C   2. C   3. B   4. A   5. B

1.3

1. "Fossil Fuel"   4. "Climate Change"
2. "Fossil Fuel"   5. Both
3. Both

2.1

1. obvious   2. warm
   massive   energetic
                 thick

2.2

1. limit   3. signs   5. escapes
2. link   4. evidence

3.1

1. Do you think   4. may not
2. might   5. couldn't
3. will

3.2

1. since   3. as
2. As a result, 4. Therefore,

PART 4

Answers will vary. See the scoring rubric on page T-69.

UNIT 10

1.1

C

1.2

1. B   2. D   3. C   4. A   5. D

1.3

1. Both   3. Both
2. The United States 4. Singapore

2.1

1. punishment   3. violence   5. forgiveness
2. innocence   4. justice

2.2

1. D   2. B

2.3

1. E   2. A   3. C

3.1

1. has abolished
2. have waited OR have been waiting
3. have believed
4. have been
5. have watched OR have been watching

3.2

1. Singapore has strict laws, so tourists should read about them before they visit.
2. States give killers the death penalty, or they give them life sentences.
3. The United States has executed 1,099 people since it legalized the death penalty in 1976. OR
   Since the United States legalized the death penalty in 1976, it has executed 1,099 people.
4. The death penalty is legal in Brazil, although it is rarely used there. OR
   Although the death penalty is legal in Brazil, it is rarely used there.
5. There is always controversy when the death penalty is discussed in the United States. OR
   When the death penalty is discussed in the United States, there is always controversy.

PART 4

Answers will vary. See the scoring rubric on page T-69.

NorthStar 3 Achievement Test Scoring Rubric: Writing

Score	Description
5	A response at this level contains relevant information from the test reading passage; the information is generally coherent and connected and is marked by several of the following: • adequate organization; effective use of transition words and phrases to display unity and progression of information • a clearly identifiable introduction, body, and conclusion although the introduction or conclusion might need more development. There is a main idea and multiple supporting sentences per paragraph. • consistent, generally correct use of word order, pronouns, relative clauses, modals, and auxiliary + main verbs; sentences often include multiple clauses or subordination • appropriate use of a variety of vocabulary items from the unit • several language errors throughout
4	A response at this level contains relevant information from the test reading passage; the information is somewhat coherent and connected and is marked by several of the following: • somewhat adequate organization; there is generally effective use of transition words and phrases to sequence and organize information • a clearly identifiable introduction and body, but a conclusion may not be clearly identifiable; there is a main idea and multiple supporting sentences per paragraph • consistent, generally correct use of subject-verb agreement, pronouns, relative clauses, infinitives, modals, and simple verb tenses • appropriate use of a variety of vocabulary items from the unit • several language errors throughout
3	A response at this level contains relevant information from the test reading passage; the information is not coherent or connected and is marked by several of the following: • somewhat adequate organization; there is a somewhat effective attempt to use transition words and phrases to sequence and organize information • more than one paragraph; there is a main idea and multiple supporting sentences per paragraph • consistent, correct use of subject-verb agreement, pronouns, relative clauses, infinitives, modals, and simple verb tenses • appropriate use of a variety of vocabulary items from the unit • several language errors throughout
2	A response at this level contains some information from the test reading passage and is marked by several of the following: • some organization; the writer is just beginning to use transition words to sequence information, but more practice is needed • only one paragraph; there is a simple main idea and several supporting sentences • generally consistent, correct use of subject-verb agreement, pronouns, relative clauses, infinitives, modals, and simple verb tenses • appropriate use of several vocabulary items from the unit • several language errors in paragraph
1	A response at this level contains little information from the test reading passage and is marked by several of the following: • a lack of organization of information • several complete sentences; there is a simple main idea and few supporting sentences • generally consistent, correct use of subject-verb agreement, personal pronouns, WH- relative clauses, and simple verb tenses • appropriate use of 1–2 vocabulary items from the unit • numerous language errors per sentence
0	A response at this level contains very little information from the test reading passages and is marked by several of the following: • very little organization of information • few complete sentences to form a short paragraph; an inadequate attempt to provide a main idea and supporting sentences • somewhat consistent, correct use of subject-verb agreement and simple verb tenses • inappropriate use of vocabulary from the unit • numerous language errors per clause A response at this level might also be blank.